# Thinking God

# Thinking God

Owen F. Cummings
Andrew C. Cummings

WIPF & STOCK · Eugene, Oregon

THINKING GOD

Copyright © 2011 Owen F. Cummings and Andrew C. Cummings. All rights reserved. Except for brief quotations in critical publications or reviews, no part of this book may be reproduced in any manner without prior written permission from the publisher. Write: Permissions, Wipf and Stock Publishers, 199 W. 8th Ave., Suite 3, Eugene, OR 97401.

Wipf & Stock
An Imprint of Wipf and Stock Publishers
199 W. 8th Ave., Suite 3
Eugene, OR 97401

www.wipfandstock.com

ISBN 13: 978-1-61097-682-4

Manufactured in the U.S.A.

# Contents

Introduction / 1

1. Why Believe? / 2
2. Why Believe in God? / 16
3. Thinking About God / 35
4. Why So Many Religions? / 46
5. Why Evil and Suffering? / 58
6. What about Indifference to Religion? / 75
7. Is There Life After Death? / 88
8. Science or Religion? / 106

# Introduction

THERE ARE many books in the market introducing students to topics in the philosophy of religion and/or philosophical theology. What makes this particular book different? First, the book is written by father and son. Such books are relatively rare. Second, the father is a theologian and the son is a philosopher. Both teach at the same institution, Mount Angel Seminary, and while they share a common background in Catholicism, their approach is ecumenical, drawing upon many Christian traditions, and they come at the things of the faith from different vantage points. While the faith remains the same, the approaches they take invite different kinds of insight. No attempt has been made to harmonize matters of style, methodologies, or ways of thinking. This is quite deliberate. The hope is that the reader will realize that different approaches to similar topics will be both complementary and enriching. Third, the table of contents attempts to straddle contemporary issues in the church and in society generally alongside more traditional topics in the philosophy of religion. Finally, the book is short. That means that it can be used for an adult study group in theology or philosophy of religion, as an introductory textbook in college, or as a textbook for seniors in high school serious about the study of religion. Andrew has authored chapters 2, 5, 7, and 8, and Owen chapters 1, 3, 4, and 6. Each chapter is intended to introduce the reader to the topic in question. It is in no way intended to be exhaustive. Both authors hope that their approaches to the topics will whet the appetite of the readers to continue to read, to think, and to probe these important questions.

# 1

# Why Believe?

*If he is not to be convicted of special pleading or of belonging to the intellectual equivalent of a holy huddle, the theologian must take his place on the common ground of intellectual learning, teaching and research.*

—George Pattison[1]

*We are, in fact, each one of us, intolerably complex: confused, bewildered, bombarded by discordant signals and demands, subject to conflictual desires and motives, unstable moods and fragile loyalties; driven by insecurity and ineffectively smothered by fear.*

—Nicholas Lash[2]

---

1. George Pattison, *The End of Theology and the Task of Thinking About God* (London: SCM Press, 1998), 6.

2. Nicholas Lash, "On Learning To Be Wise," *Priests and People* (October 2001): 358.

## ORIENTATION

Why believe? Why believe in a religion, or in a particular worldview for that matter? How do we know what's true and what's not? Isn't it a matter of opinion since there is no universal acceptance on most issues that are of real human significance? The material in this chapter may be somewhat discomfiting as it moves towards an initial discussion of the nature of truth. Most people, including students of theology, experience a degree of frustration, at times tending towards a judgment of irrelevance, when it comes to more obviously philosophical matters of epistemology and truth. Those who specialize in these foundational aspects of philosophy and theology sometimes write in a language that is far from accessible, even to the philosophical or theological initiate. To help lever us into the chapter let us spend some time thinking about the orientation quotes at the beginning. They will provide us with a nuanced platform from which we may launch our exploration into "Why believe?"

For theologian George Pattison, in speaking about faith, the theologian must be able to speak intelligibly to his peers and contemporaries in language they can understand. Unless this can be achieved, believers indulge themselves in religious positivism, requiring no intellectual underpinning whatsoever. Theology becomes almost a private language with no bridges or connections with the ordinary language of the public forum. For theologian Nicholas Lash, it is more than attempting to articulate our religious point of view in ways that are intelligible to the general public. Lash acknowledges that it is not just about being reasonably clear. We are not discarnate intellects articulating truth in perfectly clear and distinct ideas, in objective and value-free language. On the contrary, we come carrying a lot of baggage, emotional, intellectual, and even spiritual. So, we ought to look for the greatest possible degree of clarity without subscribing to a specious kind of objectivity. At the outset, these thinkers help us to see that we are

THINKING GOD

not dealing here with black-and-white approaches to truth, with un-nuanced avenues of "knowing" and "believing." To help us situate more carefully our question "Why believe?" some, albeit very brief, telling of the Western intellectual story seems necessary if we are to make headway in this chapter.

## FROM THE BEGINNING TO THE ENLIGHTENMENT

Although it is not possible to date with precision the emergence of human beings on this planet, it seems to be the case that from the earliest recoverable moments of human self-expression, our ancestors have cherished some kind of religious faith or other. One needs to be careful here and not claim too much. The scholar of religions, Ninian Smart, points out that "we shall never know, on purely scientific and historical grounds, what the emergence of human consciousness was really like. The evidence is gone for ever." Smart is simply stating a fact. He speculates, however, that from earliest times, when we examine "the scanty remains," "mixed attitudes," and "the complicated fabric of beliefs" of the ancients, the seeds of religious faith are present.[3] Certainly, in the ancient world of common existence between Jews, Christians, and Graeco-Roman "pagans," religion was a common bond, even if Christians in their "atheism" seemed to be undoing that bond by insisting on their God alone as real. People did religious things, participated in religious rituals, and accepted religion as part of the natural fabric of society. This remained very largely the norm in the West right up until about the eighteenth century when matters began to change.

Beginning with the Enlightenment in the eighteenth century, questioning of such traditional religious faith and practice took a radical turn. Skepticism about authority emerged, about authority of any kind—philosophical, theological, political—as people

---

3. Ninian Smart, *The Religious Experience of Mankind* (New York: Charles Scribner's Sons, 1969), 77–78.

*Why Believe?*

looked for sure and certain foundations that would match the new discoveries of science. "Think for yourself!" was the great slogan of the philosopher Immanuel Kant (1724–1804). Kant's proclamation is not necessarily bad. His cry frees us from thinking that is harmful or destructive, confining and cramped, and it frees us from superstition. It holds out a certain liberty. It would be sheer foolishness not to applaud the accomplishments of the Enlightenment. Not everything before the Enlightenment was good! John Macquarrie wryly reminds us that "there were plenty of evils in the old pre-Enlightenment days when Christianity had things all its own way and missed its chances."[4] In our post-modern world there is much reflection on the Enlightenment, pointing out its flaws and failings. Even criticism of the Enlightenment, however, seems to stem from a way of thinking espoused by the Enlightenment. This has been well grasped by the philosopher Louis Dupré: "In my opinion . . . critique of the Enlightenment continues to rely on principles inherent in the Enlightenment itself. Its summons to uninhibited critical thinking—*sapere aude*—challenges any principles that stand in the way of such a critique, including the Enlightenment's own. Formerly, few dared to turn the power of their critique on the rule of reason itself. Today's critics are prepared to do so, though the source of the critical impulse lies in the very movement they criticize."[5] If the Enlightenment gave us modernity, the critics of post-modernity are using the same Enlightenment-given tools to make their critique of the Enlightenment. Perhaps most critics might agree that the major Enlightenment flaw was to equate thinking *for* yourself as thinking *by* yourself, to isolate one's thinking from tradition, tradition understood broadly as conversation with others, past and present.[6] Simply put, it is impossible to free

---

4. John Macquarrie, *Invitation to Faith* (Harrisburg, PA: Morehouse Publishing, 1995), 9.

5. Louis K. Dupré, *The Enlightenment and the Intellectual Foundations of Modern Culture* (New Haven and London: Yale University Press, 2004), 335–36.

6. I owe this distinction between "thinking for yourself" and "thinking by

one's own thinking from the thinking of others, both past and present. Even if the word "tradition" carries too much freight for some people, the reality behind it, that is to say the thinking of other people, is impossible to avoid. It is there, recognized or not.

## HISTORICAL CONSCIOUSNESS, PLURALISM, AND THE FREE MARKET OF IDEAS

Cardinal Avery Dulles suggested that there have been three primary consequences of the Enlightenment for Christian faith: historical consciousness, pluralism, and the free market of ideas.[7] First, the development of historical consciousness, that is to say, that people at any given time in history have but a partial access to truth, and indeed, that the understanding of truth is formed and molded by the cultural presuppositions of any given period. Each idea, each person, *is* a history, and not only *has* a history. Second, pluralism is the recognition that there are many different and often competing ways of understanding reality. The benefit of pluralism is a respectful tolerance among people of differing views. The downside of pluralism lies in a pervasive sense that it is impossible to know the truth in any clear way. The recognition of many options, of many ways of understanding reality, may "make any particular commitment more difficult if not weaker."[8] Third, is the free market of ideas, a phenomenon closely related to pluralism. Just as we are surrounded in the West with a free market of goods and services answering to every conceivable human need and at times every imaginable human vice, so we are also provided with a free market of ideas through instantaneous and omnipresent information about everything. The benefit here is incremental knowledge leading to genuine enlightenment about so much that

---

yourself" to my co-author, Andrew Cummings.

7. Avery R. Dulles, *The New World of Faith* (Huntington, IN: Our Sunday Visitor Publishing, 2000), 14–16.

8. Ibid., 15.

is important and that impinges on our lives. At the same time, there is real loss from this free market of ideas. A person may feel so entirely overwhelmed with philosophical and religious choice, as it were, that she succumbs to the notion that personal temperament and individual taste determine the nature of truth.

These three primary consequences of the Enlightenment have contributed to a contemporary crisis of religious faith, as people struggle with the questions: "Is any worldview really true? How do I know?" Such deeply existential questions have led for some to a real crisis of religious belief and decline in religious practice. It is difficult not to agree with John Macquarrie when he says, "The past two hundred and fifty years have been marked by a steady decline of religion in the West and a corresponding growth of secularism."[9] Macquarrie's judgment seems to be more true of Europe than it is of the United States where active religious practice remains very high, and the question of secularism/secularization takes us into murky waters where both sociological data and philosophical reflection throw up different possible points of view. Having made these various admissions and acknowledgments, probably few would deny that the question, "Why believe at all?" presents itself in a very compelling way for people today, and it is a question that we must face as Christians.

## WHY ARE WE?

Is there any absolutely final, absolutely clear, and absolutely objective meaning to human existence? A very difficult and disturbing question! John Macquarrie writes: "No one can prove beyond doubt either that there is a meaning and purpose to human life, or that there is no such meaning and purpose. Here believers and agnostics are in the same boat."[10] I think Macquarrie is right. If

9. John Macquarrie, op. cit., 3.
10. Ibid., 4.

such purely objective meaning were available, it would seem to follow that all reflective human beings would espouse the same basic perspectives, and clearly they do not.

It may, however, be possible to make a beginning of an answer to the question, "Why are we?" Immediately there comes to mind the great question put by the philosopher Leibniz, the question surely that is the ground of all metaphysics: "Why is there anything rather than nothing?" That is the more objective and less personal form of the question, "Why are we?" or, "Why am I?" Thinkers put it in different ways. The Oxford Anglican philosophical theologian, Austin Farrer, is reported by John Macquarrie as having put it like this: "As I once heard Austin Farrer say, in a typically Oxonian way, 'It seems terribly odd that we exist.'"[11] This is probably not our preferred form of expression, but most people from time to time come up sharply against this question about the meaning of personal existence, perhaps most often in boundary situations like the death of a loved one, or some other deeply troubling crisis in life. The Catholic apologist, Michael Novak, on the other hand, takes Farrer's "oddness" and gives it a much more positive spin: "The wonder of it all is that there *could* have been nothingness. Instead, the world came to be—this is the first of wonders! Those who say that there are no miracles overlook existence."[12] Existence itself is miraculous. It may help to point out that the word "miracle" derives from the Latin verb *mirari/*"to wonder." Existence, my existence, at least on occasion, excites a genuine sense of wonderment. We feel the compelling power of the question, "Why are we?" even though absolutely clear and objective answers elude us.

In some way, however, we may be said to provide an answer to the question in the very shape and texture of our lives. We are actually living an answer to the question, even if just implicitly.

---

11. John Macquarrie, *Two Worlds Are Ours: An Introduction to Christian Mysticism* (Minneapolis: Augsburg Press, 2005), 25.

12. Michael Novak and Jana Novak, *Tell Me Why* (New York and London: Pocket Books, 1998), 20.

While it may be the case that absolute truth as a present possession does not and cannot exist, that we live in a world of "irreducible diversity in orientations to life and of chastened pretensions to universal and unconditional truth," nevertheless the decisions and choices we make in life seem to point in some specific direction.[13] Indeed, the decisions and choices we make might be construed as acts of faith, acts of faith precisely because the truth of these decisions and choices cannot be absolutely established beyond any shadow of doubt. Of course, that is not the same thing as saying that such truths upon which we base our lives cannot be established as reasonable, nor that we cannot demonstrate that some truths are more persuasive and compelling than others. We make decisions, enter into conversations and discussions, and live our lives as though some positions or truths had a much greater claim on us than others. Scientist Chet Raymo is surely correct when he writes: "If every idea has equal currency in the marketplace of ideas, then truth becomes a matter of whim, politics, expediency, or the tyranny of the strong."[14] Philosophical theologian, Hugo Meynell, makes the same essential point: "If anyone does not maintain that her own beliefs are rationally defensible, she is dishonest. If she thinks that they are not only rationally defensible, but of some importance and value, she will be blameworthy if she does not try to show their reasonableness and value to others."[15] The refusal to recognize this position seems to me sheer irrationalism. So, our question, "Why are we?" or "Why am I?" is evolving fast into the

13. Kathryn Tanner, "Why Are We Here?," in *Why Are We Here?* ed. Ronald F. Thiemann and William C. Placher, (Harrisburg, PA: Trinity Press International, 1998), 5.

14. Chet Raymo, *Skeptics and True Believers* (New York: Walker and Co., 1999), 68.

15. Hugo A. Meynell, *Is Christianity True?* (Washington, DC: Catholic University of America Press, 1994), 1. See also Meynell's excellent *Postmodernism and the New Enlightenment* (Washington, DC: Catholic University of America Press, 1999) where many of the ideas in this chapter are teased out with reference to the key philosophical figures in postmodern philosophy.

questions, "What is truth? How do I know?" In answering these questions world, self, and language come into "endless interplay," but it seems we need to provide some sort of defensible and credible position.[16]

## REALITY, KNOWING, AND TRUTH

There are many and complex philosophical positions in the endless interplay between world, self, and language, and it is no part of this book to enter into the intricacies of the philosophies of knowledge. Listen to what Nicholas Lash has said: "Each of us comes from somewhere: from some particular place, some tribe, some set of stories . . . Truth is tradition-dependent, and learning how to speak the truth takes time."[17] What I want to do is, accepting the basic position of Lash, set out in summary-form a position on reality, knowing, and truth, and then try to make a brief, reasoned defense of it.

1. Reality is what is.
2. What is, is what is said to be in a true judgment.
3. A judgment is true when it has raised and answered satisfactorily all the relevant questions so that,
4. Truth lies in judgment and nowhere else.

This position on reality and truth seems to me so obvious that I cannot think of a way to disagree with it, without in fact demonstrating it! If I disagree with it, then I am making a judgment that the position is not true. I am insisting necessarily that "truth lies in judgment and nowhere else." The criterion of a judgment's truth is the degree to which every pertinent, every relevant ques-

---

16. David F. Ford, *Theology, A Very Short Introduction* (Oxford: Oxford University Press, 1999), 156.

17. Nicholas Lash, *Holiness, Speech and Silence: Reflections on the Question of God* (Burlington, VT and London: Ashgate Publishing, 2004), 61.

tion, has been asked and answered. Of course, there may be other questions to be asked and answered that have not occurred yet to the inquiring subject. This means, therefore, that every judgment deemed to be true is true in a *virtually* unconditioned way, not in an *absolutely* unconditioned way. There is a radical humility in this approach to truth. Nonetheless, the uncomfortable questions arise: Have we now voided the notion of "absolute truth" altogether? Without wanting to, have we sunk into a morass of relativism?" I don't think so. Rather, in positing a judgment as true, we are *intending* absolute truth. The judgment will be maintained until further relevant questions may demonstrate its inadequacy and consequently require its revision in some respect. Absolute truth is intentional rather than a total and present possession.

More often than not, this tiered approach to reaching the truth, or what might be called "the virtually unconditioned," takes place rapidly, perhaps at times instantaneously, especially when it has to do with fairly obvious matters of fact. When, however, it comes to matters where interpretation plays a more substantive role, the process is more laborious and drawn out, and this is the case with philosophy and theology. Few have provided a clearer understanding of what is involved in interpretation than David Tracy: "To give an interpretation is to make a claim. To make a claim is to be willing to defend that claim if challenged by others or by the further process of questioning itself. When there are no further relevant questions either from the text or from myself or from the interaction that is questioning, then I find relative adequacy. I then present my interpretation to the community of inquiry to see if they have further relevant questions. They often will."[18]

We might refer to the approach adumbrated here as a hermeneutical approach to truth. The radical humility implicit in this view in no way demands the subject to capitulate to alternate views. On the contrary, it acknowledges the demands of dialogue, it calls

---

18. David Tracy, *Plurality and Ambiguity, Hermeneutics, Religion, Hope*, (Chicago: University of Chicago Press, 1987), 25.

upon a defense of positions—that is, it requires apologetics in the strictest sense of the word—it insists upon the agony of inquiry, and it eschews any form of arrogant and intolerant complacency. This is far from easy since we tend to be impatient of reasoned learning and debate, and that takes time. I become in practical terms a dialogical believer. "If I am a dialogical believer, I know that my present state of knowledge is imperfect and incomplete, but that does not inhibit me from offering the best interpretation I can of what is available to me, and being prepared to apply that interpretation as best as I can in my own circumstances."[19]

## TEMPERAMENT AND TRUTH

There is another important dimension to the notion that truth is tradition-dependent, and that is the fact that human beings are different temperamentally, and temperament or personal orientation affects how we approach matters of truth. It has been suggested, for example, by historian John O'Malley, that there are four basic cultures in the West, four basic modes of Western intelligence: prophetic, academic, artistic, and humanistic.[20] Each of these cultures or modes of intelligence has its own particular approach to truth. The prophetic mode is marked by protest, a certain contempt for the world, reform, and utter commitment on the part of the prophet. It is the culture of the martyr and the fanatic. It refuses negotiation and abhors seeking common ground for fear that the truth may be diluted or relativized. Its style is that of "the shout, the proclamation, the lament, the command, the bark, the paradox . . ."[21] The academic mode is what we typically associate with academics, that is, a relentless intellectual pursuit of the truth through the raising of questions. O'Malley offers this description of the

19. George Pattison, op. cit., 35.

20. John W. O'Malley, *Four Cultures of the West* (Cambridge, MA: Harvard University Press, 2004).

21. Ibid., 12.

academic style: "That style is the analytical, questing and questioning, restless and relentless style in which we in academe are today immersed. It is the style of learning that is never satisfied, that is critical of every wisdom, that is insatiably eager to ask the further question, and that is ever ready to propose yet another perspective. It is the style of learning that is almost by definition agonistic and contentious. It is the style that holds in highest honor sound argument."[22] Next comes the humanistic mode, which privileges literature and poetry as the primary vehicles of truth and insight. It stands in stark contrast to the academic culture. Thus, "In poetry the reasons of the heart prevail, in a form of discourse that is more circular than linear. If culture two seeks clear-cut definition, this culture, at least in this particular aspect, glories in ambiguity, in rich layers of meaning."[23] Through these rich, humanistic layers of meaning we catch glimpses of truth, not least the truth about ourselves. Finally, there is the artistic mode which has to do with physical beauty. It is the culture of dance, painting, sculpture, music, architecture, and human ritual. It has to do with non-verbal communication of truth.

Temperamentally and psychologically, in terms of our own particular journeys through life we shall find ourselves located predominantly in one of these four cultures. O'Malley writes: "I take it as axiomatic that the more fully individuals fit the definition of one culture the more intolerant they are of the other cultures or at least the more uncomprehending . . . The four cultures are grounded in human beings, with their likes and dislikes, their fears and hopes—with their mothers and their fathers and their styles of upbringing."[24] Clearly, it follows that there will be clashes and tensions between these four different approaches to truth-telling. It is no less equally obvious that each of the cultures intends truth, so that, in O'Malley's terms while they may be rivals they are also

22. Ibid., 11–12.
23. Ibid., 15.
24. Ibid., 27, 34.

siblings.[25] If they are siblings, they bear a family resemblance to one another, and they may get along as conduits of truth without the evil of mutual excommunication. Catholicity in truth demands as much.

## CONCLUSION

Why believe? Every human life, as we have seen, represents an implicit but real answer to the question. Every human life represents in its own way a "virtually unconditioned" judgment of truth. But there is always so much more, the further relevant questions that are all around us in our contemporary society flooded with an overwhelming excess of knowledge about everything. For a dialogical believer, necessarily belonging to one of the four cultures of the West, listening becomes a priority virtue, a listening that extends throughout the entirety of one's life and, indeed, one's day. This is not a listening that is limited to *academe*. Listening in the sense being used here is a listening after wisdom, a virtue that is permeative of all authentic living. Satirist and author, Tony Hendra, makes this comment: "The only way to know God, the only way to know the other, is to listen. Listening is reaching out into that unknown other self, surmounting your walls and theirs; listening is the beginning of understanding, the first exercise of love." He learned the importance of the virtue of listening from an English Benedictine, Dom Joseph Warrilow, OSB, his spiritual mentor. Dom Joseph said to Hendra: "None of us listen enough, do we dear? We only listen to a fraction of what people say. It's a wonderfully useful thing to do. You almost always hear something you didn't expect."[26] I have no doubt that some readers will have experienced a degree of disquiet in reading this chapter. This is

---

25. Ibid., 26.
26. Tony Hendra, *Father Joe: The Man Who Saved My Soul* (New York: Random House, 2004), 181.

the paschal dimension of philosophy and theology. If the approach to the question, "Why believe?" is uncomfortable, the reader is invited to struggle towards an alternative that will yield a higher and more satisfactory viewpoint. Now, however, we pass on to the more specific question of believing in God.

# 2

# Why Believe in God?

> *Against the proofs of God's existence it is also said that they do not lead to inner and strong conviction. The proofs leave us cold, for we are dealing with objective content and can see well enough that if this is the case, then so is that, but the insight remains something external only.*
>
> —Hegel, *Lectures on the Philosophy of Religion*

THE TITLE of this chapter, "Why Believe in God?" contains an immediate and important ambiguity, and one which is reflected in the quotation from the German philosopher Hegel at the top of this page. This ambiguity consists in what has often been noted as the difference between "believing *that* something is the case," and "believing *in* something." If I believe *that* something is the case, then I am claiming that it is a *fact*. I am claiming that there is an objectivity to it, a facticity that is non-negotiable, that remains the case whether anyone anywhere likes it, is interested in it, or even cares enough to notice it. Presumably, for instance, the world was factually round well before anyone tried to establish it as a fact, and (as we know from the stir it created in certain circles) regardless of how it managed to upset people. On the other hand, to believe *in* something suggests a kind of investment of personal value. Although such a value may be connected to something factual, the believing *in* aspect of the situation is not reducible to a fact. Thus, such a phrase as "I believe in myself," with the attendant self-confidence which that statement implies, may of course suggest the factual existence of a self to believe in; but to believe *in* that self is to do more than simply announce its factual status. It is to announce rather that one's self is an object of positive value, in which one has a certain investment. Now, clearly, much more remains to be said about these two phenomena of "believing that" and "believing in," but the general point is probably clear enough for now.

The point of these remarks is to draw attention to the difficulty involved in asking the question "Why believe in God?" For, according to the above-mentioned ambiguity, it could be construed as a question about the factual basis for believing in God, or it could be seen as a question about one's decision to make an investment of personal value in God. It seems to be difficult to separate these two interpretations of the question. For if you talk to the average religious person, who certainly has a value investment in God, it would seem strange to hear him say, "Yes, I believe in God, although I don't think he exists." In this sense, the *value* that one finds in God *builds* upon the (merely presupposed) *fact* that God exists. On the other hand, a religious person would usually not think that God was just one more fact amongst a world of facts—they would probably insist that God, if indeed he factually exists, has to be a fact of a quite special/extraordinary kind, worthy of inspiring the devotee to *believe in* him.

Yet, in asking the question "Why believe in God?" one dominant approach—that of natural theology—has been to address the factual basis for belief in God. Natural theology is usually seen as the study of the nature and existence of God, his attributes, and relation to the world. This kind of study is centered on the notion of facts, since its practitioners think that anyone can come to a certain knowledge of its principles just by using their reason. In this sense, natural theology is usually distinguished from revealed theology, which is thought to require a special appeal to some form of revelation (in Christianity, fundamentally, this would be the scriptures). The truths and insights that come from revealed theology may well make sense, they might be true, and they may even form a body of systematically connected knowledge—but they cannot be claimed to be "facts" in precisely the same way that natural theology can lay claim to the status. Quite simply put, revealed theology cannot, while natural theology can, demonstrate its claims by appealing to principles that any rational person can accept, regardless of "religious affiliation."[1]

In order to answer the question "Why believe in God?" attention must be given to the afore-mentioned factual dimension of natural theology; yet the valuational element of belief in God cannot be left out of the picture. In this chapter, I will offer a defense and explanation of an approach to God based in natural theology. But I will do more. The chapter will finish with a suggestion for understanding the link between believing *that* God exists, and believing *in* God. It will be seen that they are not quite as far removed as might be supposed. However, a properly balanced answer to the question of "Why believe in God?" must await the chapter on "the problem of evil." For it is only there that the valuational side of belief in God comes to the fore and provides an adequate philosophical response. While this chapter will focus on the factual grounds for believing that God exists, the chapter on the problem of evil will complement this account by delving into the valuational grounds behind our making a commitment, which we call "believing in God."

An answer to the question posed by natural theology, "Why believe in God?" will be provided in three stages. Firstly, I will be-

---

1. Although this is not a denial of their ultimate demonstrability. Thomas Aquinas argues that the principles of revealed theology, whilst not demonstrable to *us* (and hence not obviously "facts"), are nonetheless factual since they come from God himself, who *can* see their demonstrability/factual status. See *Summa Theologica*, Part I, Question 1, Article 5.

gin by providing a basic concept/definition of what we mean when we say "God." Without this, it is not clear how we can even ask for a reason to believe in "God," since we just won't know what we mean. Secondly, I will offer one of the traditional arguments for the existence of God, which has become known as the ontological proof.[2] This argument provides some insight into what a claim about the "factual" status of God could mean. Finally, I will make some suggestions about how this investigation into the factual status of God's existence can link up with the obvious valuational investment that most religious people have in God. Since much of what Christians identify as directly valuable in the God that they believe in is revealed in scripture, the link that I will try to make is tantamount to arguing for a connection between revealed theology and natural theology—or, in the language that I have been using—between "believing *that* God exists," and "believing *in* God."

## A CONCEPT OF "GOD"

Since it is impossible to begin from nowhere, I admit a certain bias in presupposing familiarity with what we have come to call the Judeo-Christian view of God.[3] But it is necessary to dwell on this point. Although from a philosophical perspective, it is useful to begin with a rough concept of what we mean by the term "God," it is simply never true that philosophy begins in midair, as it were. Although it is not always the cause for humility that one would expect, philosophy always presupposes a whole realm of ideas, views, and discourse before it begins the business of think-

---

2. Other arguments, just as forceful, can certainly be offered. I make no judgment on the superiority of this proof of God—I simply like its simple structure, which makes it ideal for beginning students in philosophy.

3. For a short, concise discussion of the influence/non-influence of Christian bias in philosophy, see Ralph McInerny, *Characters in Search of their Author* (Notre Dame: University of Notre Dame Press, 2001), 3–15.

ing things through. The philosopher, before he or she begins to philosophize, is first and foremost, a human being, brought up in a world brimming with already-existent ideas, information, and opinions. Before one can discuss the concept of ethics, there is already an ethical realm; before one can talk about the justification of knowledge, one "knows" and makes knowledge-claims all the time. To miss this point is, as Hegel pointed out, like assuming that the biological process of digestion first requires an intimate knowledge and study of biology and the digestive tract. In terms of our own project, the point is that if we are searching for a rough definition/concept of God, then it is natural to look to the religious tradition within which "God" first became a meaningful reality.[4]

In terms of our own philosophical project, it would seem that the Judeo-Christian notion of God, at the very least, must be that God is: (i) the *source* for the whole of reality—in religious language, this is often expressed in the language of *creation*; (ii) absolutely *unique*—we have a sense of this attribute from scripture, where God is often called "jealous," and where we even find a commandment that Israel is to have no other God but he.

Let us adopt these two principal elements of the concept of God and see how they affect the investigation into the question "Why believe in God?" In dealing with the factual side of God's reality, natural theology allows itself to be guided by these religiously based insights. In the first place, if we are looking for the source of our world and reality, a world itself filled with facts, then this source, if it exists, must itself be factual. That is, it is not possible to explain that the facts of this world have their source in something that is utterly non-factual. More technically, there is a

---

4. It is arguable that the contemporary tendency is to assume that any investigation into "God" as meaning something like "ultimate reality/first principle" is an issue that stands free from any traditional religious association. However, regardless of the truth/falsity of this position, it remains equally the case that long before this philosophical position was even developed, religious tradition was the main source of the notion of "God." At any rate, it is not so very easy to separate the philosophical and religious realms of discourse.

vague awareness in the religious idea of God as source, that there cannot be anything in reality that is not present preeminently in God. Thus, for example, if you begin, as natural theology does, by emphasizing a factual dimension of reality—say, the fact that our world is filled with causes and effects—then it is only fitting that the source of this causal reality must itself be causal—in this case, something like, "first cause." The point here is that natural theology, in dealing with the factual side of God, takes up the religious idea of God as source, and expresses it as a "factual source"—without necessarily stipulating in advance which factual dimension this source is to account for.[5] Secondly, natural theology takes up the religious idea of God as *unique*. And again, since it trades in the factual reality of God and his attributes, this uniqueness must be factually expressed. This point is perhaps more difficult to grasp. It could be explained as follows: Although it is true that God must be the factual source of reality; he cannot just be "one more fact" alongside all the others. If he were, then he himself would be equally in need of a source, just like all the other facts. No, God, as the factual source of reality, must equally be the *unique* factual source of reality.[6]

At this point we have more or less arrived at a rough concept of God. For the philosophical purposes of natural theology then, we can define God as the unique source of the whole of reality. The next step is to address the factual side of God. The question to be answered next is "Why believe *that* God exists?" The traditional reasons and arguments given to answer this challenge have conveniently been called proofs for the existence of God. There are a

5. So, each of Aquinas' "five ways" can be seen to take up a particular portion of our factual reality—causal, contingent existence, actuality, teleology, goods—and push on to a proof of its source—a source which itself will be factual and explanatory of those facts with which we began.

6. The philosophical danger of putting God alongside other facts was called memorably "Onto-theology" by Heidegger, and, in his language, amounted to forgetting the distinction between "Being" and "beings" (in the language I am using, this would be a forgetting of the distinction between the "Factual Source" and "facts").

number of different types of proof, and even a number of versions for each one. However, all of them aim to *factually* establish/prove the reality or existence of God. Since there is not time to cover all of them, I have selected Anselm's ontological proof, which will be examined in the next section.

## ANSELM'S PROOF

St. Anselm's proof for the existence of God can be set out as follows:

1. We have an idea in our minds of God as, by definition, "that than which no greater can be conceived."
2. To "exist in the mind" and to "exist in reality" are not the same thing, but . . .
3. It is greater to exist in the mind *and* reality, than in the mind *alone*.
4. If God (that than which no greater can be conceived) existed only in the mind, then it would be possible to conceive of something greater than God (i.e., which existed not only in the mind but in reality as well)—but this is not possible: for then, "that than which no greater can be conceived" would be "that than which (at least one) greater can be conceived." This is a contradiction.
5. So, that than which no greater can be conceived (God) must exist both in reality and the mind.

Such is Anselm's argument, and as the voluminous secondary literature attests, the real work begins in trying to comprehend exactly what he meant! An attempt will now be made to clarify his argument, and in two stages. In accordance with the two religious attributes of God mentioned above—God as *source,* and God as *unique*—I will first of all try to explain how Anselm's argument demonstrates *that* God exists as the factual source of all reality.

And secondly, I will explain how, within the structure of his argument, God can be seen to be *unique* amongst facts.

## GOD AS SOURCE

Natural Theology, as we have seen, attempts to demonstrate the notion of God as source, but crucially, in a factual manner. Thus, it is not enough to see the proof as plausible or likely—either it succeeds in proving that God exists or it does not. Now, returning for a moment to the religious notion of God as source of all reality, we could convert the religious talk of creation into philosophical guise, by saying that there is nothing in reality outside of God. In our thinking about God, there is simply nothing of which we can conceive that is external to God. If we could conceive of some bit of reality external to him, then to that extent he could not be its source. This much indeed is directly implied by the religious notion of creation. But it is an important first step in understanding Anselm's proof. For if we begin to see that God has nothing outside of him, then this is also to recognize that, in this same respect, God has no *limitation* on his reality—for if there were a bit of reality for which God was not the source, then he would be *limited* to being the source for everything else. And now we come upon the meaning of Anselm's description of God as "that than which no greater can be conceived." Anselm's description of God is simply this same notion of "unlimitedness" in God, although this time in more general terms than his status as source. Anselm asks us to think of God as unlimited, in *anything* that we think about God. Perhaps an analogy would help to clarify this point. Try thinking about the spatial Universe we live in as somewhere, somehow, reaching a limit. At that point, supposedly, if we were able to travel right up to it, we would come across some kind of a limit, some sort of barrier. But then, as everyone knows who has thought at all about this, the obvious difficulty arises about what lies beyond the limit. More space? Nothing? And if so, what would the "nothing" be like! The difficulty that the mind has in trying to conceive of a spatial limitation to the Universe is analogous to the difficulty Anselm sees in trying to think of any limitation in the concept of God (who, recall, would be the very source of any Universe).

Having recognized the meaning of Anselm's description of God as that than which no greater can be conceived, let us deal with the case of someone who tries to conceive of God as "only an idea in the mind." This kind of position, Anselm thinks, would be characteristic of the atheist or agnostic, neither of whom deny that there is some kind of concept/idea of God—even if, as they might say, it is highly doubtful that it exists, or even is no better than wishful thinking. Anselm argues that, although it is certainly true that theist and atheist alike can have this concept of God in their minds, the difference enters with the word "only"—as "God is *only* an idea in the mind." For this is a clear limit-word. The atheist (or "fool" as Anselm more uncharitably puts it) is doing the logically impossible. He is trying to limit the illimitable. He is attempting to take the concept of God as "beyond any conceivable limitations," and then to limit its status to an idea in the mind. In short, Anselm thinks that the impossibility of saying that God, who is beyond limitations, is limited to an idea in the mind, shows that he cannot just be an idea in the mind, but must exist in reality too. In this sense, to say that it is greater to exist in reality and the mind, than in the mind alone, is tantamount to saying that it is "less limited." It is like saying that it is greater to be a human than an animal—for a human has all of the main biological attributes of an animal (sensation, mobility, reproductive capability) but additionally, reason. To put it the other way around, to be an animal would be to be more limited, because of the lack/absence of reason—the animal would be *limited* to all the attributes a human has, other than reason. On Anselm's model, existence in reality would also be to exist

*Why Believe in God?*

as an idea in someone's mind,[7] but with *more* to it—a *greater* reality—namely, "existence in reality."

Before moving on to a consideration of how Anselm's argument establishes God as unique, it must again be asked, in what sense has Anselm succeeded in proving *that* God exists? The answer to this is basically that he has established the impossibility of conceiving God not to exist. In other words, Anselm's proof works somewhat indirectly, in something like the following way. Suppose there are two possibilities: x and y. One of them must be true. Now, we can know with certainty that y is false. What follows? x of course. Anselm has shown that since the concept of God is beyond conceivable limitations; and since either God is a mere idea or he is both an idea and a reality; and since for God to be only an idea is an inconceivable limitation; therefore the opposite possibility is true—God must exist both as idea and reality. And it is important to see the full import of this: God *must* exist both as idea and reality, according to Anselm. This is why his argument falls so clearly into the discipline of natural theology. That is to say, into the realm of facts.

## GOD AS UNIQUE

Now, amongst the many attacks and criticisms that Anselm's argument excited, none is as famous as the so-called "lost island" passage, which came from Gaunilo himself, a monk and contemporary of Anselm. Gaunilo tries to show that Anselm's ontological argument can be taken and applied to almost any idea that we have of anything, thereby "proving" it into existence. Anselm's argument, by proving too much ends up proving nothing. Consider the case of a lost island, lying somewhere in the ocean, and possessed of all manner of superb qualities. Let us call it "that island than

---

7. To see this point, just try thinking of some really existent object of which you have no idea—as soon as you start speaking of it, you have an idea of it! Even if it's a fairly uninformative idea, at least at the beginning.

which no greater can be conceived." Then, says Gaunilo, since it is greater to exist in reality and the mind, than in the mind alone, the idea that we have of this lost island cannot *just* be an idea—the island must exist in reality! Not surprisingly, Gaunilo takes this to be an absurd conclusion, and it is difficult not to agree with him. So what has gone wrong with Anselm's argument?

The first point to be made is that Gaunilo's challenge to Anselm's argument works along the lines of a *parody*.[8] By supposedly reduplicating Anselm's reasoning about God onto the case of the lost island, Gaunilo hopes to show us that the absurdity of our conclusion shows that the argument itself is flawed. Thus, since Anselm is using that same argument to prove the existence of God, Anselm's version of it must also be flawed. This in turn means that the only way that Anselm can convincingly defend himself against Gaunilo's parody is by arguing that there is an important difference in his argument about God which Gaunilo fails to capture in his attempted parody about the island. Anselm must tell us how his argument about God is significantly different from Gaunilo's parody about the island. Anselm does in fact say in reply to Gaunilo that his reasoning applies only to God, and I will shortly go into the reasons for him saying so. However, it is crucial to understand one more point about the Anselm-Gaunilo dispute. Since God is reputedly *unique* amongst all "objects" of our experience—indeed so much so that some philosophers are uncomfortable with even using the word "object" here—then any way of thinking about God which undermines this uniqueness would thereby seem to cast doubt on whether we really are talking about "God" here. Clearly, if Gaunilo's parody works, then "God" is on a par with anything else that you might, in a jocular moment, wish to "prove" into existence—say, Pegasus, Mickey Mouse, or the present king of France. Yet, if God is just one more object, with no obvious difference to any other, then there can obviously be no uniqueness to him. My point here, is that in showing how Gaunilo's parody does not work,

---

8. From a purely logical point of view, it is a *reductio ad absurdum*.

## Why Believe in God?

Anselm would also be showing how his own thinking about God establishes the status of God as somehow unique.

Having highlighted what Anselm must accomplish in defending his ontological proof, it remains to see how he does so. Why exactly is it the case that Gaunilo's island parody does not work? Anselm must give us something about the definition of God as "that than which no greater can be conceived" which is different to the island definition as "that island than which no greater can be conceived." The difference in Anselm's definition of God can be seen as follows. Doubtless it is true that, should one choose to think of the greatest conceivable island, it would follow that it exists. However, there is nothing stopping us from conceiving of the island than which only one greater can be conceived; or perhaps the island than which only ten greater can be conceived. That is, there is nothing in the concept of "island" which bars us from thinking of these possibilities, even if one of the possibilities is thinking of the very greatest conceivable island. Now, compare this situation to the definition of God. Is it possible to think of the God than whom only one greater can be conceived? No. Quite simply put, this would be trying to think of "that than which no greater can be conceived, than whom only one greater can be conceived"! If we understand Anselm's definition of God as beyond any limitations, then it makes no sense to speak of God as with at least one limitation, i.e., having one greater than he. But this still does not give us an adequate difference between Anselm's argument and Gaunilo's parody. One more step must be taken. It is as follows. Although *if* one chooses to think of the greatest conceivable island, it will follow necessarily that it exists in reality; this is only a conditional necessity—that is, no necessity at all. In other words, since you can well think of an island that which only one greater can be conceived (which would not necessarily exist in reality), to argue Gaunilo's island into existence involves the *choice* to think of the greatest conceivable one. God however, whose existence follows from his nature as greatest conceivable, cannot not be thought as the greatest conceivable (on pains of not really understanding his nature). Either you understand God's nature as defined—in which case you see that he exists—or you do not understand God's nature as defined, which unfortunately means only that you are no longer talking about God, and hence cannot even speak about his existence or non-existence. Ultimately, this means that the necessity of God existing in reality is an unconditional necessity, not, as in the case of Gaunilo's island, a conditional necessity. Now, since it is the case (it can be tried out with any object, not just lost islands) that no other object other than Anselm's God can have such an unconditional necessity of existing, this means that Anselm's argument is incapable of being properly parodied by Gaunilo. This of course means that Anselm's way of thinking about God still manages to uphold his uniqueness.

At this point then, it can be seen that Anselm's ontological proof rests on two key suppositions, each of which in turn arises out of the very soil of the Judeo-Christian understanding of God. Firstly, the notion of God as the Creator or Source for the whole of reality, involves thinking of God as beyond any conceivable limitation. This point is central to understanding how Anselm's definition of God, as that than which no greater can be conceived, works. Secondly, the notion of God as somehow unique is also seen to be central to his argument. There must be a truly significant difference between God and all other objects, and this difference must be reflected in the way that we think about God. Gaunilo, who tries to apply Anselm's thinking about God to other imaginary objects, understands the importance of this concept of uniqueness, and thinks that Anselm's argument does not pass the test. As we have seen however, Anselm's argument contains within its own implications, the explanation for why Gaunilo's challenge cannot work.

## THE POINT OF ANSELM'S PROOF

Even if one has been following the reasoning up to this point, even if one accepts the force and cogency of Anselm's argument, one could still shrug one's shoulders, and say "So what?" Is Anselm's proof of God's existence more or less the same as, for example, the proof of a mathematical theorem? If so, then we can expect that most people will show a comparable amount of enthusiasm about it. So the question to be faced is about the significance or point of this argument. Is it only important for someone who already believes in God?[9] Or does it claim to somehow have a built-in appeal for anyone who understands its meaning? I believe that it is the latter.

But let us approach this question carefully. What is at stake here? Often an answer is not forthcoming because the question is not clearly stated. In this case, it would seem that most people, in addition to the factual, demonstrative aspects of a proof for God's existence, are also expecting to be presented with something which resembles the kind of worship-inspiring God, who stirs devotion in people's hearts, and who comforts people in desolation. A tall order for a proof.[10] But whether or not such an expectation is justified, it seems to be the underlying supposition that leads people to say "So what?" when presented with a proof for God's existence.

In order to see how the proofs are relevant, it is therefore necessary to say something more about the surrounding context

---

9. Karl Barth argued for this interpretation in his *Fides Quaerens Intellectum* (London: S.C.M. Press, 1960). For a reply to Barth, and opposing view, see M.J. Charlesworth, *St. Anselm's Proslogion* (Oxford: Oxford University Press, 1965).

10. For an interesting discussion of this issue, see Ralph McInerny, *Characters in Search of their Author*. The author argues that people simply expect too much from proofs for the existence of God. Indeed, he maintains that it is tantamount to a confusion between theoretical and practical reason—the former capable (as are the proofs) of delivering disinterested objective conclusions; and the latter which is capable of somehow perceiving a good and acting towards it.

of belief in God, and perhaps more importantly, how that belief is related to our more common, everyday beliefs. In line with this, it is helpful to turn to the level of everyday, common objects. Take the notion of our loved ones—people who are loved and valued by us. Apply the two elements which were utilized in the ontological proof, *factual existence* (although this time not in terms of "the source") and *uniqueness*. The factual existence of those whom we love is not so very hard to grasp. Maybe one of the main differences between it and the factual existence proved of God, is that we cannot "prove" it in the same sense. We could of course point to them and say "Look!" "See?" But this is not exactly a "proof" in the philosophical sense, even if everyone believes that it is a perfectly acceptable indication of the fact. Yet, the factual existence of our loved ones is quite basic to our experience. If we had been searching for a lost loved one, then it would not be enough to be presented with photos, letters, voice recordings—we would require their actual physical presence/factual existence before us. Clearly, on the level of common experience, our relationship to loved ones is heavily tied up with their factual existence.

But next we turn to the notion of uniqueness. In what sense is a loved one "unique"? What I wish to argue here is that in loving a person there is an at least implicit belief in that person's uniqueness. This is backed up by even the most mundane examples. A genuine love between a man and woman is often taken to imply that no one else will do for either of them. If one of them is too easily "replaceable" by someone else, this is tantamount to admitting that there was nothing unique about that person, and this is often taken to be proof that there was no genuine love there in the first place. Again, if parents have a child who dies, then in so far as that child was really loved, it should be apparent to all (and the parents most of all) that it could never be replaced. Never. Seeing a loved one as somehow unique, is, I maintain, essentially part of what constitutes a love relationship. Moving on to more explicitly philosophical territory, there are some fascinating discussions in

*Why Believe in God?*

the works of Plato and Aristotle concerning the nature of love and the merits of a loved one. Indeed, it seems that there has been a philosophical discussion of love from the beginnings of the western intellectual tradition. Yet, many philosophers are not entirely satisfied with what this Platonic-Aristotelian tradition has said. For there is a tendency there to focus on the specific *qualities* of a loved one, or even the *type* of person whom one loves. The issue could easily become then, whether the loved one is loved either (i) for themselves, idiosyncratically; or (ii) for qualities which they embody. The real difficulty seems to be that, if you claim the first option, then you are declaring a love with no basis. When asked, that is, why you love person x, you would reply, "I don't know. I just do." This is not particularly satisfying, since in that case you might have loved them purely by dumb chance/luck—and no one really trusts either chance or luck to remain constant. On the other hand, if you claim that you love them because they are kind, generous, and intelligent—then should someone else come along exemplifying to a higher degree those same qualities, it is only to be expected that you would switch them for your erstwhile loved one. In both cases the uniqueness of the loved one, as loved, is threatened.[11] Now, regardless of how this dilemma is resolved, it should be clear at this point that the quality of uniqueness is somehow centrally involved in loving someone, as can be illustrated both from common observations and philosophical investigation. The point of all of this is to make clear that there are plenty of examples from everyday life, of how we love people who both factually exist and whom we see as unique. Indeed, that in the case of uniqueness, there is an especial relevancy. So then, how can it be the case that God, who has been proven to be *factually existent* and *absolutely*

---

11. For a concise discussion of some of these concerns, from a contemporary philosophical perspective, see the article by Bennett Helm, in the Online Stanford Encyclopedia of Philosophy http://plato.stanford.edu/entries/love/#6. The 'non-fungibility' of love is the expression used there, rather than uniqueness.

*unique*, could still nevertheless, fail to be an object of concern/relevancy to so many people?

There is another way of looking at the situation. Perhaps the real problem consists in a superficial view of God on one side ("up in heaven") and humanity on the other side ("down here on earth"). If one begins with this view, then everything which "moves" us and is of ultimate concern to us will be in "our own" realm. This leaves us trying to understand how we can "connect" our feelings of love and value to the transcendent God on the other side. But what if God were present in each and every thing and person which was of genuine value/worth? What if, in loving the people that we love and celebrating the things which are of value to us, we were *already*, in principle, acknowledging the goodness and presence of God? This is actually what I take to be the case, and there are strong precedents in philosophy for viewing God this way.[12] But if this is true, then it follows that proving God's existence and uniqueness, followed by the puzzlement of why this proof should fail to impact people, is confused on principle. God has already been "moving" us, has already been present to us in everything good we experience. What we term "proof for the existence of God" simply attempts to get a handle on this ubiquitous presence of God. But, it might be asked, what point would a proof serve, if everyone was already in the midst of God's presence?

Taking our modified view of God as already present in our experiences of good things/value/love, why should it have occurred to someone to raise the question of God's explicit existence/reality, distinct from other things in the first place? To answer this requires again, modifying the question. For if God is already there, then to explicitly raise the question of his distinct existence can only mean to ask about the *continued* reality of God. The reason why a proof for the existence of God should have originally occurred to someone, is that God is so closely tied to our experience

---

12. In Augustine, Anselm, and even Thomas Aquinas (cf. the 4th way, on how all the good things imply an ultimate good as their cause).

of value/goodness, that when our experience of value/goodness appears to dry up/run into trouble, we are left wondering whether there is any "ultimate reason/ground" for it. That is, we are wondering "Where did God go?" The certainty and demonstrative aspects of a proof for the existence of God can then be seen as a tapping into our already puzzling experience of goodness and value, and as attempting to provide some kind of security. In other words, while our particular loved ones and experiences of love and value might seem to be fleeting, we wish to have some sort of assurance of a ground/foundation of what we love and value—and a foundation which is certain, abiding, and which will not change with the passage of time. Perhaps an analogy will help. Under normal circumstances, for someone to show you that a window in your bedroom opens to allow you to climb through it into the garden, may or may not be interesting—but most likely, you will dismiss it the next moment (as you would with other supposedly trivial knowledge such as that there is an extra lock on the door). However, should you be trapped in a house-fire, unable to escape through the normal means, this knowledge and its basis in fact, would suddenly become very significant indeed. The factual existence of the window and its properties was already there all along, but its real utility might not have become apparent until desperate circumstances. In parallel fashion, the proofs for the existence of God must be seen against the backdrop of an already existent God. The reason why such proofs seem powerless is because they are viewed abstractly, without paying attention to the real importance of their object.

In essence it is being suggested here that the proofs for the existence of God are an unfolding of a God who is *already there*. Until it is made clear how God is already there in love/value/goodness, it will be unclear both why it should matter and why he should exist or not, and therefore in what sense the proof is more than an abstract intellectual exercise. It has already been pointed out that even within the confines of the concepts used in, for instance, Anselm's proof, there is more than a passing connection between the ways in which we think about our loves, and the kind of exercise that the proof is (i.e., the notion of uniqueness as centrally constitutive of the experience of loving). One way of looking at this situation is that the proofs for the existence of God—indeed the very importance of a God at all—are often not recognized until people are struck dumb with suffering. And then, in line with the view of God as "on the other side," it is asked how he could exist in the face of the breakdown of goodness—all the while ignoring the idea that God was primordially experienced *in* the goodness. The aim of this chapter has been to provide an argument for why we should believe *that* God exists, factually, as well as providing some suggestion about how such arguments can be seen to matter. Or, in the language I have been using, why the proof *that God exists* should be connected to the issue of *believing in God*, as the full locus of our values and commitments.

# 3

# Thinking About God

*If you have understood, then it is not God.*

—St. Augustine, *Sermon* 117.5

THE WORDS of St. Augustine that open our chapter are salutary. They are salutary not only for theologians but for anyone trying to think seriously about God. The meaning behind the words is that one never gets to the point where one can say with complete conviction, "Now I've got it! Now I have a comprehensive understanding of God." The fourth-century Cappadocian theologian, St. Gregory of Nyssa, coined a word for this unending search to understand God. He called it *epektasis,* which we might paraphrase as constant "straining forward on the upward climb that never stops."[1] One never reaches a final point of understanding. This has been a leitmotif in the history of Christian reflection on God. It is found both East and West, in the Scriptures, in patristic and in medieval theology, in the theology that has emerged in and after the sixteenth century, and in contemporary theology. Despite this traditional emphasis, it would be true to say that a large number of

---

1. Frances M. Young, *Brokenness and Blessing* (London: Darton, Longman and Todd, 2007), 20.

people do not feel the need to strain forward on the upward climb towards an understanding of God. Too often there is a contentment to rest passively with an understanding that is nothing short of mediocre. "Many people who would not dream of relying on the understanding of literature or the sciences they acquired as children are content to leave their juvenile theological convictions largely unexamined."[2] These are the words of the spiritual writer Kathleen Norris. They ring true. They ring true not just of people in general, as it were, but also of people who have had the opportunity and privilege of years of higher education. Sometimes when such educated persons turn their hand to the critique of religion, the understanding of God and of the things of God which they entertain, is juvenile indeed.

This is the case, for example, of Richard Dawkins, the scientist whose book *The God Delusion* has received such massive public exposure and acclaim.[3] In his sustained attack on religion and especially on Christianity, he reveals himself as holding what can only be called "juvenile theological convictions." There is no felt need in Dawkins for *epektasis* of any kind. He certainly has not informed himself of the multiple studies in theology, and indeed, interdisciplinary studies, that go far beyond juvenile convictions about God and religion. The literary critic Terry Eagleton writes that Dawkins on theology is like "someone holding forth on biology whose only knowledge of the subject is the *British Book of Birds*."[4] The theologian Nicholas Lash comments that "One cannot imagine a physicist holding an atomic particle, or a zoologist a yak, with the same sustained contempt and loathing, the same cavalier disregard for accurate description, the same ignorance of the literature, with which Dawkins treats all religious beliefs, ideas

---

2. Kathleen Norris, *Acedia and Me* (New York: Riverhead Books, 2008), 114.

3. Richard Dawkins, *The God Delusion* (London: Bantam Press, 2006).

4. Terry Eagleton, "Lunging, Flailing, Mispunching," *London Review of Books*, vol. 28, no.20, October 19, 2006.

and practices."[5] Dawkins maintains that he is attacking not just any particular version of God or gods, but all gods or God, however they are understood.[6] However, his own particular version of God or gods bears little or no resemblance to the understanding of reflective believers.

What exactly do we mean by "God"? How do we reconcile what we know to be "true" from our culture with our convictions about "God"? It seems to me that both questions are fundamentally important. The first one invites an understanding of God that is congruent with the received tradition of Christianity. The second one forces us to relate that to our actual and living circumstances today. This means that there is a correlation of a kind between the two questions, and it will not do to attempt an answer to one but not the other.

Ideas of God that flow from reflection on certain human experiences point to the reality of God, but without grasping or comprehending the reality. Since all human language necessarily structures and expresses our experience and understanding of the things of the world, what we might call creation, when language is applied to God, who is not a thing of the world, not creation, that language can be applied only in a metaphorical or analogous way. Herbert McCabe, the Thomist theologian, had a neat way of expressing this conviction when he said that all language for God is "second-hand clothing": "We always do have to speak of our God with borrowed words; it is one of the special things about our God that there are no peculiarly appropriate words that belong to him . . . He is always dressed verbally in second-hand clothes that don't fit him very well. We always have to be on guard against taking these clothes as revealing who and what he is."[7] Second-hand

---

5. Nicolas Lash, *Theology for Pilgrims* (London: Darton, Longman, and Todd, 2008), 4.

6. Richard Dawkins, op. cit., 36.

7. Herbert McCabe, O.P., "God," and "The God of Truth" in *God Still Matters* (London and New York: Continuum, 2002), 3.

clothing is not made-to-measure, but is ill-fitting, and yet it sort of does what needs to be done. All language for God is like that. It does not fit, it cannot fit the reality of God, but it sort of does what needs to be done to avoid saying nothing at all. Language for God must be understood metaphorically, not literally.

Metaphors for God are drawn both impersonally and personally. For example, impersonal metaphors include "a mighty Fortress," "light," "a rock of refuge," and so forth. Personal metaphors include father, mother, husband, king, lord, and so forth. Given the patriarchal culture that produced the Hebrew Scriptures and the New Testament, it is hardly surprising that the majority of personal metaphors are masculine rather than feminine. While that is understandable, it becomes problematic "if male figures predominate to such an extent that God somehow appears to be more appropriately represented as male rather than female."[8] While we have no access to God other than through images, no image is ever entirely adequate and always represents to some extent a distortion. There is no way to the reality of God except through the image we have of God, and that image is always to some extent a distortion. This is why the *Catechism of the Catholic Church*, for example, insists upon purifying images of God: "We must continually purify our language of everything in it that is limited, image-bound or imperfect, if we are not to confuse our image of God—'the inexpressible, the incomprehensible, the invisible, the ungraspable'—with our human representations. Our human words always fall short of the mystery of God."[9] While we may, as the Catechism encourages, constantly purify our images of God, it is extremely difficult to see how we can quite get beyond these images. There simply is no other way to think of and to speak about God, and indeed, to pray to God. At the same time,

---

8. John H. Wright, "God," in *The New Dictionary of Theology*, ed. J. A. Komonchak, M. Collins, and D. A. Lane (Collegeville: The Liturgical Press, 1987), 426.

9. *Catechism of the Catholic Church*, 42.

if our faith is to mature, there needs to be some element of critical reflection about God and God's action in our human regard that is found to be satisfactory, even if it is impossible to reach absolute satisfaction.

One such critical reflection is provided by John H. Wright. John H. Wright has proposed a three step pattern that may be discerned in divine and human interaction. The first step is God taking the absolute initiative. This is God creating out of pure love and gratuitousness, the reason there is something rather than nothing. This is God's grace at work and is antecedent to any response. The second step is the response of the human creature to this initiative of God. Whenever a human being acts freely she or he is aligning self with God, or is departing in some measure from God. It should be pointed out that this response of the human creature to God may, in fact, be anonymous in respect of God. God is always known, but not always named and recognized. The third step is God responding to the creature's response to the divine initiative. God is affected by the action of his creatures. Wright points out that these three steps should not be thought of simply in terms of chronological succession, though time is obviously involved. The steps represent an analytic interpretation of divine-human interaction. "The future does set before us the initiative of God's love and the past embodies the divine judgment, but at all times in the present, God is here in gracious love, inclining and illuminating the created agent, and the free creature is more or less accepting the gracious love of God (or refusing it), and God is responding in effective judgment. In this way God is profoundly immanent in our lives and in the whole course of human and cosmic history, guiding events and accomplishing his gracious purpose."[10]

This reflective interpretation, however, is not the way everyone thinks, and is not the way everyone images God. Here is what I mean. In 1949, the American Trappist theologian, Thomas Merton, wrote the following words: "I never had an adequate

---

10. John H. Wright, op. cit., 434.

notion of what Christians meant by God. I had simply taken for granted that the God in whom religious people believed and to whom they attributed the creation and government of all things was a noisy and dramatic and passionate character, a vague, jealous, hidden being, the objectification of all their own subjective ideals."[11] One suspects that many contemporaries would share views like this. Such views have passed into our culture from the world of psychology and ultimately from the world of philosophy in the person of Ludwig Feuerbach. God is simply a projection of our own subjective ideals and needs.

What are some of these common distorted images of God? Pulling examples from different authors and sources we might compile the following list.

First, God as cosmic moralist. Behind this image lies the idea that since God is the divine lawgiver and judge, he keeps careful records of all human offenses, and ultimately will punish offenders. Needless to say, there is a far more positive association of God with morality than this, but it is a fairly common distorted image. Second, God as controlling power. This image understands God as determining every detail of the world. Not just the large details, as it were, such as a tsunami, or an earthquake, or other such natural phenomena, but the small details too, such as God's choosing to take a particular life at a particular time. Undoubtedly, the various Christian traditions have nuanced and sophisticated ways of thinking about God's power, but at the popular level this notion of God as controlling power is widespread. Third, God as sanctioner of the *status quo*. This is the God understood as the protector and custodian of the way things are. The present order is provided by God and protected by God. It is divinely willed and to challenge it is to challenge God. Here again one may find sophisticated versions of this image, but crudely presented, it is simply unacceptable. The reason is that the *status quo* too often is disin-

---

11. Thomas Merton, *Elected Silence* (London: Hollis & Carter, 1949), 138–39.

terested in the promotion of a more just and equitable social and political order. A God who was the custodian of an unjust social order, however defended by the pundits, would be no God at all in the Christian sense. Fourth, God as male. At least in Christianity there is a very long-standing tradition of thinking about God in masculine terms, as already noted. Obviously, Jesus of Nazareth was a man. However, the other two Persons of the Trinity are also thought of in male terms: God the "Father" obviously so, and the Holy Spirit is often spoken of as "he." Many thoughtful Christian thinkers no longer find this a helpful way of talking about God. Alternative ways of speaking about God and to God have not met with universal acceptance at this point. A greater degree of tolerance among Christians is required here. There is no room for an unreflective or positivist dogmatism that in principle disallows any change from Scriptural ways of speaking about God.

## FINDING OTHER WAYS

Arguably, the most precious experience and value that human beings have is love. It hardly needs to be pointed out that "love" has been rendered banal, superficial, and cheap in so many different ways in our culture. Love is best understood as a process of self-donation to another person. Calling love a process moves us away from seeing it simplistically as one experience or as one action. It is much better thought of as a sequence of experiences or actions. Describing love as self-donation means that love is about literally giving oneself to another. This giving may take a variety of expressions. Each expression, however, is intended symbolically to stand for one's entire self. In saying authentically to someone "I love you," one is intentionally saying to the other, "All that I am and all that I have is for you."

In the first letter of St. John this is how God is described: "God is love, and those who abide in love abide in God, and God abides in them" (1 John 4:16). In so far as it is possible to speak of an essence of Christianity, it seems to me to be this, that God is Love, that God is the unbounded, unconditional, eternal Process of Self-Donation. "Love" is God's best name, we might say. Thus, to say "God is" is to say "God loves." Probably many Christians would ally themselves with this way of thinking. To interiorize this conviction is difficult and takes time, a lifetime. The theologian James T. Burtchaell has it right when he says: "There is nothing very astonishing about a God who loves us relentlessly, except that we generally do not believe in one."[12] It is not particularly astonishing to claim that God loves humankind relentlessly. The claim is based as we have seen both in human experience and in the text of the New Testament. What happens, however, is that experiences and false understandings and interpretations, inculcated over perhaps a long period of time, get in the way of appropriating the deep meaning of this claim. The way a person is brought up, the way in which one is educated and nurtured, all affect how one thinks of and how one images God. Let us illustrate this from the poetic work of the Anglican priest-poet, George Herbert (1593-1633). The first poem to which I wish to draw attention is called "Discipline":

> Throw away thy rod,
> Throw away thy wrath:
> > O my God,
> Take the gentle path.
>
> For my heart's desire
> Unto thine is bent:
> > I aspire
> To a full consent.
>
> Not a word or look
> I affect to own,
> > But by book,
> And thy book alone.

---

12. James T. Burtchaell, CSC, *Philemon's Problem* (Grand Rapids: Eerdmans, 2001).

Though I fail, I weep:
Though I halt in pace,
        Yet I creep
To the throne of grace.

Then let wrath remove;
Love will do the deed:
        For with love
Stony hearts will bleed.

Love is swift of foot;
Love's a man of war,
        And can shoot,
And can hit from afar.

Who can scape his bow?
That which wrought on thee,
        Brought thee low,
Needs must work on me.

Throw away thy rod;
Though man frailties hath,
        Thou art God:
Throw away thy wrath.

The first thing to notice about this poem is that it is a prayer addressed to God. Brought up in a household and in a tradition in which God was thought of as angry, Herbert encourages God to throw away his rod and his wrath, to throw away his anger, and to take the gentle path. He acknowledges his sinfulness, he weeps for his sins, yet he still creeps to the throne of grace. He recognizes in the penultimate stanza that the Love of God, the Love that *is* God is the motive for the Incarnation—"that which wrought on thee, brought thee low." He recognizes further that the same Love, we might say the same God, must work on him. And so in the last stanza, Herbert once again invites God to throw away his anger. One can hear Herbert struggling in this poem/prayer to shed the dysfunctional image of God as angry and to reach towards the life-giving understanding of God as Love.[13]

    13. See *Heaven in Ordinary: George Herbert and His Writings,* edited and introduced by Philip Sheldrake (Norwich: Canterbury Press, 2009), 29, 58.

## THINKING GOD

Sometimes one hears it said that an emphasis on God as Love is insufficiently demanding from a human perspective. Very easily, it is alleged, this viewpoint could lead to a theological sentimentality. That is of course possible. At the same time, it needs to be emphasized that, understood at its best, this emphasis on God as Love is supremely demanding. Writing about the experience of falling in love, the Irish poet Michael O'Siadhail says that love is "Gratuitous, beyond our fathom, both binding and freeing."[14] In the poem from which this line is taken, "Out of the Blue," O'Siadhail is putting into words his meeting with the most important person in his life, his wife Brid. Notice each word in O'Siadhail's description of his love with Brid: gratuitous, fathomless, binding, freeing. Love is gratuitous, something unearned and undeserved, simply given, without condition. Love is fathomless, cannot be measured or quantified. Love is binding, that is to say, there are duties and obligations that arise out of this process of self-donation, especially for fickle human beings. Love brings its own discipline. Finally, love is freeing. The freedom that flows from genuine love is a freedom to flourish as who one is, giving oneself unreservedly to another. O'Siadhail is speaking of love between two people, his wife and himself. May we not use his understanding for our response to God as Love? There is no sentimentality here. If God indeed is Love, that demands of me the deep recognition that Love is gratuitous, fathomless, binding, and freeing. There is a lifetime of conversion in those words. That conversion may be understood as a lifetime's struggle daily to answer these questions: "Do we wake up every morning amazed that we are loved by God, aware that this is the ultimate in delight, dignity and self-worth? Do we allow our day to be shaped by God's desire to relate to us? Are we ready to be stretched in our hearts, minds, imaginations, actions and sufferings in order to do justice to this glorious God? Do we habitually see ourselves, other people

---

14. Michael O'Siadhail, *Poems 1975–1995* (Newcastle: Bloodaxe Books, 1999), 124.

and creation in the light of God's desire for us all to flourish? Do we simply long to enjoy God?"[15]

Struggling daily to answer these existentially demanding questions of God helps flawed human beings move towards a more integrated and accepting view of themselves. Simultaneously, the questions push us towards seeing God as one who loves unconditionally, who is not "bored, disgusted or impatient with anything he has made, even when we have made a mess of it for ourselves."[16]

---

15. David F. Ford, *The Shape of Living* (London: HarperCollins, 1997), 28.
16. Rowan D. Williams, *Tokens of Trust* (Louisville-London: Westminster John Knox Press, 2007), 55.

# 4

# Why So Many Religions?

> *We need to steer around the dangerous path of imagining that God plays favorites, that God favors or has 'chosen' Jews but not Egyptians, or Christians but not Muslims, that in general God has revealed himself to 'us,' but not to the 'others,' to Paul on the way to Damascus but not to the rest of the Jews who stuck with the Torah, that God prefers men to women in order to do 'His' work, or white people to black, or Western Europeans to Asians, or has in some way or other granted special privileges to a particular individual or nation, race or gender—or planet or galaxy!—in a particular time and language, that has been withheld from others.*
>
> —John D. Caputo.[1]

IT IS difficult to disagree with these opening words of the philosopher John Caputo. In our post-colonial world nothing less will do. Nevertheless, his remarks seem to rule out the particularity and specificity of what Christians have come to call "revelation." If the absoluteness of the revelation in Jesus Christ is compromised, then Christianity, at least as traditionally understood, loses its integrity and identity. Somehow the absoluteness of Jesus Christ

---

1. John D. Caputo, *On Religion* (London and New York: Routledge, 2001), 113.

must be maintained while also at the same time acknowledging with Caputo that God does not play favorites. In this chapter the allied questions are briefly tackled: "What is religion?" and "Why are there so many religions?" The first question will unfold through an examination of some of Caputo's ideas, while the second question of its nature invites a greater degree of speculation.

## WHAT IS RELIGION? DIALOGUE WITH JOHN D. CAPUTO

Staying with the thought of John Caputo we might open up the answer by saying: "by religion . . . let me stipulate, I mean something simple, open-ended, and old-fashioned, namely the love of God."[2] The one who loves God is religious. One feels the persuasiveness of this statement—if a religion is not about the love of God in some obvious sense, it has no human value—but it requires further probing. So, continuing with Caputo's agapeic thinking: "The opposite of a religious person is a loveless person. 'Whoever does not love does not know God' (1 John 4: 8). Notice that I am *not saying a 'secular' person . . . Some people can be deeply and abidingly 'religious' with or without theology, with or without the religions. Religion may be found with or without religion.*"[3] This is surely right. If religion is about loving God, then the non-religious person is strictly the loveless person, not the so-called secular person. God may be known by those who love without necessarily being named.

That raises the further question, however, of the purpose of institutional religions. If religion is about loving God, and the human heart knows how to love, what is the need of institutions? Caputo provides an answer: "They provide religion with a critical mass, with a structure and social constancy without which it would likely disappear or dissipate. They provide permanent structures—

---

2. Ibid., 1.
3. Ibid., 2–3.

buildings and institutions and communities—within which the great narratives are preserved, interpreted, and passed on to the next generation. They perform innumerable acts of service and generosity and they preserve the name of God by proclaiming it and praising it systematically and consistently."[4] Religions, for Caputo, are human constructions, important human constructions, which serve to articulate the love of God, to encourage that love, and to wean humans off egocentricity and narcissism in all their seductive forms. Some speak of the great world religions as "global wisdom traditions," those traditions that make for human flourishing both individually and in community, that have been tried and trusted over centuries, and through whose multifaceted institutions wisdom is mediated. In that sense Christianity, with an estimate of about two billion adherents, may be thought of as "at present the largest global wisdom tradition."[5]

A question emerges for the Christian, and perhaps acutely for a Christian in the broad Catholic tradition: Does not the traditional understanding of "church" transcend this understanding of religion? Is not the church in some ontological sense the real manifestation of Jesus Christ in space and time? Yes, the church does perform sociologically and psychologically the roles laid out by Caputo, it is a wisdom tradition in Ford's sense, but Catholic Christians claim that it is more. The church is by God's grace, God's action, the very embodiment of Christ and so his premier sacrament or efficacious sign in the world. It is this, however, as a pilgrim people, not as a people who have arrived at their glorious destination as the self-evident luminous sign of Christ's indwelling. The church is a treasure in earthen vessels.

---

4. Ibid., 32.

5. David F. Ford, *Christian Wisdom* (Cambridge: Cambridge University Press, 2007), 2.

## SO MANY RELIGIONS

"Why are there so many different religions?" is a very complex question. If we think of religion as a multi-dimensional approach to the divine or the transcendent, then the short answer to the question lies in the freedom of the individual. Individual persons grow necessarily out of some tradition or another, but if they find that tradition religiously insufficient, and if they have enough religious imagination and creativity, they may decide to found their own religion. In this fashion, the roots of religions ultimately lie in the mysterious freedom of the human person in his or her relationship with the divine or the transcendent. This is looking at religion very broadly, of course, and if some of these "religions" have sticking power and persuasive attraction for others, then they become established.

This way of thinking leads to another allied, complex question, "Is one religion as 'valid,' as 'true,' as 'good' as another?" And for Catholics there is a further question, "What is the relationship between these so many religious 'ways' and Christianity, and ultimately the Catholic Church?"

There appear to be three basic theological approaches to the question. The first approach maintains that truth is to be found only in one religion, with all the others regarded as false. We may call this "exclusivism." Immediately, especially in today's egalitarian world, exclusivism doesn't feel right. It doesn't feel right because, whatever one's particular religious tradition happens to be, all who do not belong to it are cut off from truth and reduced to falsity. That seems both arrogant and incredible. It also seems to speak of a God who has very definite favorites, and that way of thinking about God seems too close, to say the least, to our all pervasive xenophobia and insecurities.

The second approach maintains that truth is to be found in all religions equally, one path being as valid or truthful as another. We may call this "pluralism." Often one will hear the idea that "everything is relative" or "to each his own." These are colloquial versions of pluralism. Pluralism is fatally flawed. While it has the appearance of being open ended, logically it is based on a performative contradiction. What I mean is this: when I affirm that every conceptual position is equally valid or equally truthful, I intend that particular conceptual position to be absolute. In other words, in implicitly demanding the truth of my proposition that every position is equally valid or truthful, I have in fact undermined what I am claiming by contradicting it! This is not a helpful way to proceed.

The third approach is this: the fullness of truth is to be found in one religious tradition, but rays and elements and degrees of that truth may be found in the others. We may call this "inclusivism." This seems to be what philosopher Michael Novak, for example, is getting at when he says that "every religious tradition in the world, every story of every single soul—has something to teach us. Something of God is refracted through each one."[6] This is much more helpful. It enables us with humble confidence to affirm absolutely the truth of our own religious tradition, while simultaneously recognizing that other religious traditions (and, indeed, every reflective human being) are somehow included in the truth. This position of inclusivism may yet have the feeling of superiority about it, but something like it is demanded by any and all intelligent seeking after truth.

Let's pick up for a moment the issue of "superiority," the feeling of superiority that appears to lie behind this version of inclusivism. In our culture many reflective people do not wish to be thought of as superior when it comes to matters of religion or ultimate value. Many wish to lay claim to their own religious position but without seeming to denigrate other religious positions. That is understandable in a world that has come to value equality and tolerance and a real recognition of the other. One does not need to

6. Michael Novak and Jana Novak, *Tell Me Why* (New York: Pocket Books, 1998), 49.

abandon tolerance or recognition of the other in advocating as superiorly true one's own religious position. Appropriating the logic of the criticism of the position named pluralism above will help here. Working towards a recognition of the other that goes beyond mere tolerance and moves in the direction of a religious apologetic is a good thing. It is a good thing despite the prevalent cultural sentiment that maintaining superior positions is bad.

## THINKING THROUGH APPROACH 3

So, our position is that the fullness of truth is to be found in Catholic Christianity, but in such a way that other religious traditions are caught up or associated with Catholic Christianity in different degrees of intensity. That still leaves us with the question: "Why are there so many different religions?" or "How do we account for the diversity of religions?" This is an extremely difficult question to answer. Indeed, any answer will reflect something of the "superiority" of one's own position. That is simply unavoidable. But here are some thoughts that may throw some light on this difficult issue.

First, we might say that entities that are vitally and socially significant for a given people are likely to establish themselves as symbols for the Divine or the Transcendent. Let's take just one example from nature. In ancient Egypt the sun-god, Amon and the fertility goddess, Isis, were two major symbols, "probably because the whole life of the nation depended upon the two great natural forces, the sun and the river."[7] Without the sun and the river, life in Egypt would not exist. Recognition of their importance gave rise, as it were, to their divinization. Please note that this is not the empirical observation of an anthropologist. It is the somewhat speculative observation of a Christian theologian. But

---

7. John Macquarrie, *Principles of Christian Theology*, rev. ed. (New York: Charles Scribner's Sons, 1977), 162.

it seems to make some sense. Could we go further with this line of thinking? Could we say perhaps that religious traditions shape the divine in accord with their context? Something like this seems to be the observation of the fifth-century B.C. Greek philosopher, Xenophanes, quoted by the third-century A.D. Christian theologian, Clement of Alexandria: "Ethiopians make their gods black with turned-up noses. Thracians make them with red hair and blue eyes. Mortals think that gods are born and have their own food, voice and shape; but if oxen and lions had hands and could draw or produce images like men, horses would draw the shapes of the gods like horses, oxen like oxen, and they would produce such bodies as the bodily frame they have themselves."[8] The Ethiopian context, the Thracian context, and by implication any human context projects something of itself, or something of its comprehensive living context on to the gods. This would add some degree of intelligibility to the multiplicity of religious traditions, but without rendering everything intelligible.

There are different psychological types *in* the various religions. There are types recognizable as mystics, prophets, ecstatics, revivalists, and puritans. The list is not intended to be exhaustive, but exemplary. Furthermore, with John Macquarrie we may say that "these types cut across the divisions between the great historical faiths."[9] Macquarrie attempts to extend this insight in an interesting direction. He makes this suggestion: "Perhaps there is also a psychology of groups, whole races or nations tending to have certain mental or emotional characteristics, though of course this would be only in a general way and would not exclude many individual exceptions . . . There may be a kind of normative position that is typical of the group as a whole."[10]

---

8. Cited in Frances M. Young, *Brokenness and Blessing* (London: Darton, Longman, and Todd, 2007), 47.

9. John Macquarrie, op. cit., 163.

10. Ibid.

## THE ANALOGICAL AND DIALECTICAL IMAGINATIONS

Speaking objectively, there can be no purely neutral starting-point for what might be called a typology of religions. Drawing up a typology demands making judgments, and making judgments necessarily invokes all kinds of presuppositions whose truth is not taken for granted by everyone. Speaking from an explicitly Christian point of view, perhaps it could be said that Christianity has two basic forms of the religious imagination that yield contrasting perspectives: the analogical and the dialectical. This is the language of philosophical theologian David Tracy, and is especially helpful.

By the analogical imagination Tracy means something like an emphasis on the immanence of God. In answer to the question, "Where is God?" the analogical imagination replies "Here!" In the words of Andrew Greeley who has popularized Tracy's position in a very accessible fashion: "The objects, persons and events of ordinary existence hint at the nature of God and indeed make God in some fashion present to us. God is sufficiently like creation that creation not only tells us something about God but, by so doing, also makes God present among us. Everything in creation, from the exploding cosmos to the whirling, dancing, and utterly mysterious quantum particles, discloses something about God and, in so doing, brings God among us."[11] There is a sense of everyone and everything living and moving and having its being in God. God is never distant in the analogical imagination, but always very present. The dialectical imagination is different. Here the emphasis is on the transcendence of God. In response to the question, "Where is God?" the answer is "Other than here!" Underscoring the absolute transcendence of God, the dialectical imagination is utterly opposed to what it sees as confining or imprisoning God

---

11. Andrew M. Greeley, *The Catholic Imagination* (Berkeley-Los Angeles-London: University of California Press, 2000), 6–7.

in people and doctrines or rituals. The dialectical imagination wishes to avoid at all costs idolatry, that is, substituting something or someone for the transcendent God. From this point of view "the analogical imagination brings God too close to the world and gives rise to superstition."[12] Both forms of the Christian imagination are necessary, according to Tracy (and Greeley), so that the analogical and dialectical are mutually corrective of the distortions of the Divine latent in each other. One could put it like this. The analogical imagination taken to extremes amounts to a kind of pantheism. It is an easy step from saying that God is in everyone and everything, to saying that God *is* everyone and everything. The dialectical imagination taken to extremes is not particularly different from atheism. If one is constantly stressing the transcendence of God and God's apparent absence from creation, it is an equally short step to the suggestion that there is no God. It seems to me very probable that in living religious traditions, at least for the most part, neither the analogical nor the dialectical imagination exists in a pure form. Nonetheless, from the total range of expressions of a given religious tradition, one is able to judge whether it is going in the analogical or the dialectical directions. There needs to be a mutual correctivity because humankind is so prone to bias, to excess, and to extremes. The possibility for imbalance and proportion is always present.

Commitment to God in one's own particular religious tradition with all its scriptures, doctrines, rituals, and practices does not necessarily demand the blanket condemnation of other traditions. Even as one believes that one's own position is "superior" to other positions, one may yet consider degrees of truth and insight—and could we also say revelation?—in other traditions. This position would be true, of course, for devotees of other the religious traditions. They would judge their own position "superior" to Christianity. This makes for a certain tension between the religions. However, philosophically and ethically it is better to enter

12. Ibid., 8.

into conversation with other religious traditions from the vantage point of commitment to one's own. The attempt to understand another religious tradition will necessarily affect one's understanding of one's own tradition. Mutual attempts to understand would lead at least to a tolerance between the religions of the world, and may move in the direction of much more than that. A genuine receptivity to the other might move someone from a static tolerance, as it were, to a dynamic and informed interaction. Who knows where this could lead?

## FOR A PRAGMATIC SEARCHER, JUDGING BETWEEN RELIGIONS

We have different religious traditions. We also have different Christian traditions, exemplifying in their own ways elements and degrees of the analogical and the dialectical imaginations. So is it just a matter of choosing which one you prefer in the cafeteria of religious offerings? Or are there any criteria that can be applied in choosing a religion, and, indeed, in judging the "truth" of a religion? The Scottish philosopher of religion, Ninian Smart (1927–2001), believes that it is possible to posit criteria for judging the satisfactory nature of a religion/worldview. There are six such criteria.

The first is modernism. By this Smart means a certain acceptance of the modern world, of science and technology, the capacity to assimilate new developments in understanding. Modernism is to be distinguished from fundamentalism. The fundamentalist is cut off from the flow of modernity and thinking in the sciences and in the social sciences as well as in the humanities.[13] Modernism for Smart is not a capitulation to modernity. Rather, it is an openness to appropriating what may be judged as helpful

---

13. Ninian Smart, *Choosing a Faith* (New York and London: Boyars-Bowerdean, 1995), 70.

to human flourishing in all its aspects. The second criterion has to do with the richness of spiritual experience. Does this particular religion encourage personal holiness, in the most comprehensive way as involving *all* of life, including the life of deep interiority and prayer? Or, on the other hand, does it inculcate a narrowness, a parsimonious vision? Third, is this religion open to other traditions? Is it in some measure or another inclusive? Or does it remain closed in upon itself, isolated from others, and from what they have to offer in the way of truth and life? In terms used earlier, is it exclusivist? Fourth, is this religion attractive in terms of its narrative and ritual offerings? This is the scriptural dimension and the worship dimension of religion. Do these draw the subject in, in a positive way as *tremendum et fascinans*? Do the Scriptures and the ritual patterns help to evoke simultaneously a contemplative attitude to and awareness of the divine, as well as an appropriate engagement with the world? Fifth, is it situationally relevant? That is to say, does it make sense of the sociocultural situation in which one lives, and does it make sense of one's own circumstances and experience? Finally, there is what Smart calls the criterion of effectiveness. Does this religion actually achieve what it proposes to achieve both in terms of the wider society and in terms of the individual? Is it really effective?

These six criteria are generic in nature. They do not take into account the details and intricacies of a given religious tradition. In laying them out in this way, however, Ninian Smart seems to avoid an impossible neutrality even as he endorses a certain spiritual pragmatism. Human flourishing is what counts, both individually and socially.

## CONCLUSION

In reality it is impossible to stand on some neutral platform and produce a purely objective answer to the question, "Why are there so many religions?" We have offered no real answer to that question, claiming that it cannot be answered objectively. In this chapter, however, the attempt has been made to show that it is not a matter of thoroughgoing relativism. Positions may be taken, judgments may be made, which lead to a greater appreciation of all the wisdom traditions even while one remains committed to one's own.

# 5

# Why Evil and Suffering?

*I shall know why, when time is over,*
*And I have ceased to wonder why;*
*Christ will explain each separate anguish*
*In the fair schoolroom of the sky.*

*He will tell me what Peter promised,*
*And I, for wonder at his woe,*
*I shall forget the drop of anguish*
*That scalds me now, that scalds me now.*

—Emily Dickinson

THESE WORDS have been chosen to introduce the topic of evil and suffering because they are poetical, not philosophical. Poetry is generally thought to be more emotional and it seems to capture our feelings and states of mind in a more direct way. Therefore, it is appropriate to let a poet launch our reflections on evil and suffering, since they affect everyone on a day-to-day basis, regardless of intellectual interest or ability. Philosophical reflection, although necessary at some level, tends to detach itself from its subject-matter and to approach it in a more round-about sort of a way. In fact, when it comes to the question of belief in God, we have already seen that believing *that* God exists is different from

*Why Evil and Suffering?*

believing *in* God. Philosophical proofs for the existence of God can be said to deal with the first kind of belief, and chapter 2 has examined their typical claims. However, it is time to look squarely at the issue of believing *in* God, of seeing God as the source and support of whatever we hold valuable. Although this chapter is about evil and suffering, it will be seen that one's concrete belief in a divine source of reality is what is really at stake. To put it bluntly, *can one realistically believe in God today, when there is such an obvious, shocking, and ultimately disillusioning amount of suffering in the world?*[1]

The existence of evil and suffering can be found wherever there are human beings, and this remains true regardless of cultural-linguistic background, religious affiliation, and economic status. At the most general level we are all faced with the same reality. Nevertheless, no one begins from a "neutral" perspective, and this chapter will examine some of the implications of evil and suffering for belief in God. In what follows we will consider firstly the peculiar challenge that evil and suffering pose for traditional belief in God; secondly, we will look at the various types of position that have been taken up in response to this challenge; and thirdly, a position will be taken up and defended as the most promising line of response.

I

Before we get into the details of this problem, it will be helpful to clarify a few of the key terms. Although we all deal with these phenomena on a daily basis, it is still helpful to make a few dis-

---

1. The same fundamental question about "ultimate values" can be asked by non-theists, although inevitably it will be differently colored. Thus, Albert Camus, a self-proclaimed atheist, asked a similar kind of question: "There is but one truly philosophical problem, and that is suicide. Judging whether life is or is not worth living amounts to answering the fundamental question of philosophy." *Myth of Sisyphus*, 3.

tinctions. Beginning with "evil" then, what exactly do we mean by this? We all know it when we see it perhaps, but now is the time for some clarification. In philosophical-theological discussion, it is common to distinguish "moral evil" from "physical evil." For example, if a person loses the sight in one eye, or is struck down by cancer, or perishes in a hurricane, he is normally said to be a victim of *physical* evil. Everybody seems to recognize that occurrences like these are bad, but it is also usually recognized (although maybe not at the time of occurrence!) that this is just how the world works. Disease, natural disaster, and danger are parts of life as we know it, and they always have been. *Moral* evil, on the other hand, is a different affair altogether. This involves a type of evil where someone, somewhere, is held *responsible* or *culpable* for it. Now, at some level, a morally evil action has to be done *intentionally* by someone if we are to hold that person responsible. A child who unintentionally shoots his sibling would usually not be held to have committed a morally evil action. An adult who deliberately shoots someone—say, out of a motive of revenge or anger—*is* held responsible for a morally evil action. This distinction between physical and moral evil is not just an abstract one. Think of it this way. It is bad enough that people are struck down by misfortunes and unavoidable disasters on a daily basis. But many people would say that there is something especially hard to bear about an evil which could have been avoided if people had shown just a touch more respect and concern for each other.

So much for moral and physical evil. What can be said about suffering? Again, unless people already knew in their gut what this means, no discussion would be possible. But it is useful to look for a definition of some sort, if only to see how suffering is connected to the other concepts that we will be examining. To begin with, suffering is a reality that accompanies evils of both a moral and physical kind. Sometimes one will suffer more from a physical than a moral evil (e.g., the physical evil of losing a child in a Tsunami vs. the moral evil of having a car stolen); but no matter which type is more extreme in any given case, suffering is usually a result of both types of evil. In this sense, one might say that suffering is the bottom-line in the problem of evil. After all, if we did not suffer at all, then it is not clear that we would have a concept of evil. Things would just be the way that they are, nothing more. But as everybody knows, there *is* something more. In fact, let us continue with this way of speaking about "the way things are," because arguably it provides us with the best clue to a definition of "suffering." Suffering then—at least human suffering, with which we are concerned—might be conceived as the experience of dissatisfaction with "the way things are." For when we suffer, we are aware that even if things *are* a certain way, they *ought* to be a different way. While we share the experience of "pain" with animals at the physical level, we are able to think about things and ask why they are this way rather than some other (better) way. For the sake of convenience, this distinction will be referred to as the distinction between the "is" and the "ought." Suffering, on this interpretation, would consist in our acute awareness that things ought not to be the way that they are. And since they are that way, nonetheless, we continue to suffer in the wish that they would be otherwise. In the case of a physical evil like blindness, we are aware that the way in which the eye actually *is* (in its blindness), is not how it *should/ought* to be—that is, a healthy, normally-functioning organ. With moral evils, such as cheating someone out of their property, we are aware that the way that someone *actually* behaved is not the way in which they *should* have behaved.

Having provided a rough definition of the distinction between moral and physical evil as well as of the notion of suffering, it must be asked how all of this fits in with a belief in God? After all, theists generally see God as the ultimate source/creator of all reality, including this world, with all of its suffering and evil. Does this not mean that God wanted evil and suffering in the world? If not, then why did he create things the way that they are? Sometimes these kinds of questions are raised in an aggressive way by people who are hostile towards religious beliefs. But a little reflection will show that the questions here, even if they are difficult to answer, are challenges which religious people have to accept and respond to. Even if one ignores these challenges to traditional belief in God, that is still the response that one has chosen—and significantly, the way in which one has chosen to represent the plausibility of religious belief to others. But how is one to respond to the questions about God, evil, and creation? How can one even know the kind of response to give?

One way to approach the issue is to take up again the distinction between *believing that* something is the case, and *believing in* something. A great deal of the discussion of this problem has been occupied with the first kind of belief. That is, with laying out the logical difficulties of both believing in God, and of reconciling this belief with the manifest existence of evil and suffering in the world. To be fair, this approach cannot be sidestepped, and something will need to be said about it. However, it will be argued that an adequate theistic response to the problem of evil and suffering will need to take into account the perspective of "believing in." In other words, the perspective of values, and commitment to values (in this case centering in God)—as when one says "I believe in God"—needs to figure in one's response, since the existence of evil is not only a logical problem. It is also a "valuational" problem which affects one experientially, and which threatens not just the "logical viability" of God, but the "existential possibility" of believing in God.

Let us lay out the purely logical problem of reconciling belief in God with the existence of evil and suffering in the world. Although there are different ways of expressing it, a classical formulation was given long ago by Epicurus and repeated in the modern era by David Hume. This is what Hume says:

> This is not, by any means, what we expect from infinite power, infinite wisdom, and infinite goodness. Why is there any misery in the world? Not by chance, surely. From some cause

then. Is it from the intention of the Deity? But he is perfectly benevolent. Is it contrary to his intention? But he is almighty. Nothing can shake the solidity of this reasoning, so short, so clear, so decisive, except we assert that these subjects exceed all human capacity.[2]

The attempt, often made by religious people, to respond to these kinds of objections to belief in God is usually called "theodicy." This can be understood to mean a justification of God (and belief in him) in the face of evil and suffering. The advantage of Hume's formulation of the problem lies in simplifying the nature of the difficulties, and therefore the differing avenues of response to it. So then, the challenge is clear. It is maintained that one cannot consistently believe *that* there is an all-good, all-powerful creator-God, *and* that there is evil and suffering in the world. To hold all three beliefs together would be inconsistent, or so it is claimed. It would appear that either we have to alter our understanding of God; or we have somehow to minimize/explain away the existence of evil and suffering in the world. In the next section some of these proposed solutions will be examined.

II

According to the problematic laid out in the previous section, any logical response to the problem of evil would have to either (i) deny that God is all-powerful (that is, he would like to eradicate evil, but he is unable to); (ii) deny that God is all-good (that is, although he could eradicate evil, he does not want to help us); (iii) deny that evil and suffering exist, or say at least that they are not as serious as we might think; (iv) accept that God is all-good and all-powerful, *and* that there is evil and suffering—but deny that human beings are capable of understanding God's deeper reasons for allowing things to be the way they are (that is, say that evil is a mystery). If

---

2. David Hume, *Dialogues Concerning Natural Religion*.

one is willing to alter one's beliefs in any of these ways, then one can remain "logically consistent" by maintaining belief in God in the face of evil. We will look at examples of each in turn, but I will defend the last of these positions, which unfortunately has been dismissed as "irrational" by the vast majority of philosophers.

(i) The first of the available responses would make the claim that although God is certainly all-good and all-loving, he is simply not up to the task of eradicating evil. Or, bearing in mind the creation motif, that it was not possible for God to have created a world where evil was either less or absent. At first sight, this is a shocking concession for a theist to make in any of the great monotheistic traditions. Witness the common expression for God, "the Almighty." Traditional metaphysics and theology have tended to take up the common impression of God as almighty and unlimited in every power and respect, and to defend its coherence and plausibility. Late medieval philosophy, for example, was fond of using the thought-experiment that God could have done things in any conceivable way (e.g., made murder good) that is, that there were absolutely no conceivable limits on what God could and could not have done. Obviously, this is relevant to our topic, since in that case, God might well have created a world with less, or even no significant evil in it.

So deeply entrenched is the notion of God as unlimited in power—both in scripture and philosophical reflection—that philosophers who wished to challenge it had to create practically a new philosophical approach to God. *Process thought* (inspired by Alfred North Whitehead) took up this challenge, and although it held onto a lot of the traditional approach, it modified its understanding of God as well.[3] Basically, process thinkers viewed God as affected directly by events in the world, and therefore not directly controlling everything. God was indeed the Creator, but one who had left himself open to change and vulnerable to events beyond

---

3. For an overview of how process thought has affected theology, see Robert B. Mellert, *What is Process Theology?* (New York: Paulist Press, 1975).

his control in the world. Process philosophers believed that their novel approach portrayed God as nearer and more relevant to the world and its suffering, and if omnipotence had to go, well and good. But they also believed that their approach was, logically speaking, more consistent. Charles Hartshorne commented that "it has become customary to say that we must limit divine power to save human freedom and to avoid making deity responsible for evil. But to speak of limiting a concept seems to imply that the concept, without the limitation, makes sense."[4] Clearly, Hartshorne has a low opinion of the traditional treatment of God's power, and offers a new assessment: "His power is absolutely maximal, the greatest possible, but even the greatest possible power is still one power among others."[5] Whether one agrees with the process thinkers or not, they represent a systematic, careful attempt to provide an alternative conception of God,[6] which has clear ramifications for the problem of evil.

This first solution to the problem of evil, which seeks to save belief in God by altering the notion of God's omnipotence, has also been represented at a more "human" level. In 1981, Rabbi Harold S. Kushner published a small book entitled *When Bad Things Happen to Good People*.[7] It is a poignant and direct response to the problem of evil, stemming from Kushner's own personal struggle with the death of his son, Aaron, from a debilitating disease at age 14. Rabbi Kushner thus found himself struggling at a very down-to-earth level with these same issues, and he reached a solution which is roughly in line with what the process thinkers have been saying. Taking his cue from the Book of Job in the Old Testament,

4. Charles Hartshorne, *The Divine Relativity: A Social Conception of God* (New Haven: Yale University Press, 1964), 138.

5. Ibid.

6. For a general critique of the process approach, from a traditionally-minded theist, see David B. Burrell, "Does Process Theology Rest on a Mistake?," *Theological Studies* 43 (March, 1982).

7. Harold S. Kushner, *When Bad Things Happen to Good People* (New York: Schocken Books, 1981).

Kushner says, "Bad things do happen to good people in this world, but it is not God who wills it. God would like people to get what they deserve in life, but He cannot always arrange it. Forced to choose between a good God who is not totally powerful, or a powerful God who is not totally good, the author of the Book of Job chooses to believe in God's goodness."[8] Kushner tries to rescue his faith in God by compromising on God's omnipotence, and focusing on his goodness. This, he believes, allows people to find an ongoing solace in the divine, developing a more mature and fulfilling relationship with God. By letting go of the notion of God's omnipotence, "we will be able to turn to God for things He can do to help us, instead of holding on to unrealistic expectations of Him which will never come about."[9] Kushner's book has been widely appreciated both within and without Judaism, and especially for its pastoral effectiveness. However, those of a more unbending traditional mindset will be unlikely to concede a limit to God's omnipotence.[10] What about a limit to God's *goodness*, as suggested by Hume's challenge?

(ii) Supposing that one insists on saying that God is all-powerful, and thus could have made the world a better place than it is. Then why didn't he? Is it possible that God might not be the all-good, all-loving deity that many people say he is? Again, as in the case of the charge that God might not be omnipotent, the suggestion that he is lacking in goodness will sound strange to anyone conversant with religious traditions. Indeed, things would be even worse for religious people on this account, since at least with a God limited in power, one could still trust in his goodness. But how could one bring oneself to believe at all in a God who was not all-good, and who was indifferent towards the existence of evil and

---

8. Ibid., 58–59.

9. Ibid., 61.

10. To represent a typical objection, "Does one want the fire-brigade to perish in the flames?"

suffering? In such a case, would it not be better to simply turn away from God and make your own way in the world as best you can?

As a matter of fact, the position that God is lacking in goodness often seems to be a sort of existential rejection of God in the face of evil. It is not very easy to find examples of people holding explicitly the position that God is omnipotent, and yet not all-good. Most people who reject God these days seem to do so wholesale. Here, on the other hand, we are faced with a reluctant acknowledgment of God's power, together with a rejection of him as a viable object of faith. To take up the language familiar from a previous chapter, there is a belief *that* God exists, together with a refusal to believe *in* him—that is, a refusal to see God as the reliable ground/support for our values. An example of this kind of response to the problem of evil can be found in some of the writings of Elie Wiesel. Wiesel survived the German death camp in Auschwitz and wrote-up his memories of it in *Night*, one of the truly ground-shaking accounts of man's inhumanity towards man. In one memorable scene he describes a crowd of emaciated, half-dead Jews who have gathered for prayers. It is Rosh Hashanah, towards the end of the Jewish year: "The voice of the officiant had just make itself heard . . . 'Blessed be the Name of the Eternal!' . . . Why, but why should I bless Him? In every fiber I rebelled. Because He had had thousands of children burned in His pits? Because He kept six crematories working night and day . . . how could I say to Him: 'Praised be Thy Holy Name, Thou Who hast chosen us to be butchered on Thine altar?'"[11] It is sometimes difficult in such cases to separate the pure anguish of words like these from how much the author really intends as his considered position. But this much is clear. If someone like Wiesel really means every word in this passage, then our second possible "response" to the problem of evil—limiting God's goodness—is no *solution* at all, as far as a theodicy is concerned. Belief in God can hardly be maintained with a God lacking in goodness. If we accept that "it is

---

11. Elie Wiesel, *Night* (New York: Bantam Books, 1982), 64.

given to man to transform divine injustice into human justice and compassion,"[12] then we are, after all, speaking of evil and suffering from a purely human perspective with no room for God.[13]

(iii) Hardly anyone from within the traditional metaphysical and theological tradition would have chosen one of the above two responses to evil and suffering. As one writer puts it, "If any one of these 'solutions' is accepted, then the problem of evil is avoided, and a weakened version of theism is made secure from attacks based upon the fact of the occurrence of evil."[14] In other words, the price one pays for being logically consistent in this way is a weakened theism. But it is important to recognize that such compromises, which revise the root view of God, were live options throughout the history of mankind. For instance, St. Augustine fought a life-long battle against the doctrines of the Manichaeans, who argued that good and evil were entirely separate things and that God was only responsible for the good things in creation. In one sense, as in the case of the approaches we have considered, this was a solution of sorts. It freed God from any responsibility for evil and suffering. But on the other hand, it posited a whole realm of evil and darkness which was outside God's jurisdiction—that is, beyond his power. A significant portion of Augustine's spiritual autobiography, recorded in *The Confessions*, is taken up with his reasons for rejecting such a position. For our purposes, what is more interesting is the solution which he offers in its place.

Augustine was the main figure responsible for establishing the *privatio boni*—evil as the "privation of good"—approach to evil and suffering, which has underpinned so much of the official Christian position ever since. Drawing on the philosophical resources of Neo-Platonism, Augustine set out to address the

---

12. Elie Wiesel, *Messengers of God* (New York: Summit Books, 1976), 235.

13. In fact, much of what is described as "atheistic humanism" today, amounts to this. Typical representatives speak of a much-needed human compassion, but without any reference to a God of any sort.

14. H.J. McCloskey, "God and Evil," in *God and Evil*, ed. Nelson Pike (Englewood Cliffs, New Jersey: Prentice-Hall, Inc., 1964), 61–84, 62.

following dilemma: (i) if evil was something God created, then it is real, and God is responsible for it; *or* (ii) if evil is not something God created, then it is unreal, and God is not responsible for it. Both options were unacceptable for Augustine, since he neither wanted to blame God for evil, nor did he want to say that evil was an illusion. The problem seemed to be that if evil was real in some sense, then apart from positing a separate realm for it beyond God's control (like the Manichaeans), there seemed to be no option but to trace it back to God. Augustine's approach was basically to say that although evil is "real," it is not quite as real as goodness. As he puts it, "No nature, therefore, as far as it is nature, is evil; but to each nature there is no evil except to be diminished in respect of good. But if by being diminished it should be consumed so that there is no good, no nature would be left."[15] In other words, you can speak of good things without even giving a thought to evil. But you cannot speak of evil in things without saying that its original *goodness* was lost. Hence there is a *priority* of goodness over evil.[16]

In terms of our problematic, Augustine's response to evil and suffering is to retain God's absolute goodness and power, but to claim that evil simply does not have same level of reality as goodness. It cannot therefore be traced back to God. There is, nonetheless, an additional question that can be asked here. When speaking about the human experience of suffering in the face of evil, does the lesser reality/existential status of evil imply that there is less suffering in its wake? Is the human experience of suffering any less, given Augustine's position? It seems unlikely. In this regard, any kind of philosophical-theological response to evil which

15. St. Augustine, "Concerning the Nature of Good, Against the Manichaeans," in *Nicene and Post-Nicene Fathers*, First Series, vol. 4. trans. Albert H. Newman, ed. Philip Schaff, (Buffalo, NY: Christian Literature Publishing Co., 1887.) Revised and edited for New Advent by Kevin Knight. http://www.newadvent.org/fathers/1407.htm.

16. When summarized in this way, the *privatio boni* position is not nearly up to the task of handling sophisticated challenges and objections. For an extremely detailed version of it, see *The De Malo of Thomas Aquinas*, trans. Richard Regan, (New York: Oxford University Press, 2001).

attempts to minimize it, or assign it a lesser reality that it has, is suspect.[17] Still, one might defend Augustine by pointing out that the truly crushing effect of evil can be rewritten as the opposite of his theory. That is, evils of the sort which truly wreck lives end up assigning a priority of evils over goodness. People who have been crushed by evil and suffering have faced the possibility that goodness has dried up, and that evil now has priority. So a position like that of Augustine's, which argues for a priority of goodness, is not entirely off the mark, at least in describing what is at stake. That remains so, even if it is incapable of convincing everybody at the existential, experiential level.

### III

David Hume's formulation of the problem of evil, quoted earlier in this chapter, left open another possible response to the existence of evil. Given belief in an all-good and all-powerful God, and given the existence of evil, one could always claim that "these subjects exceed all human capacity." That is, one could opt for response (iv), which is the claim that evil is a mystery. At first glance this might not appear to be a very helpful response. Some might even claim that it is a cop-out. But let us look more closely. In standard formulations of the problem of evil and belief in God, such as the one by David Hume, it is tacitly assumed that we know the possible intentions and purposes of God. This comes through when it is claimed that there is a basic *inconsistency* in believing in an all-good, all-powerful God, given the existence of evil. But might it not be the case that there are good reasons for the existence of evil and suffering which we simply fail to see? Given the weakness

---

17. There are other examples. Augustine also speaks of what might be called the "Monet" effect—looking at the "big picture," evil tends to round itself out, and to magnify the glory of God. Cruder and less sophisticated examples of this type of approach might include the Christian Scientists, who appear to deny completely the reality of pain and suffering.

and fallibility of human understanding, there is nothing bizarre in claiming that our minds are not up to a task, such as comprehending the divine purpose in creation.

That there is no logical contradiction in holding this belief can be seen in the most mundane examples. It is quite conceivable that a parent might act in ways which displease a child. The child might howl in protest, and yet all along fail to see the deeper meaning involved. For instance, opting not to buy a coveted toy on the grounds that it would be spoiling the child. Or more seriously, plunging a febrile infant into cool water to bring down the fever could be seen as cruel from the child's perspective. Admittedly, these examples might sound trivial next to the truly stunning evils of human experience. But the salient point is that unless we are privy to the entire sweep of the divine mind, we cannot claim to know his full intentions in allowing evil. A more sustained, philosophical attempt to envisage concretely what such a scenario might entail has been made by John Hick. Hick argues that the divine purpose in allowing evil and suffering in creation can, at least partially, be understood as necessary to human "soul-making." In a nutshell, the way that the world is, is suitable for "the development of the moral qualities of human personality"[18]—including such traits as compassion, solidarity, kindness, etc. None of the character traits which we admire and promote in people would have any meaning in a world devoid of evil and suffering. Even if one does not agree with Hick's position, it remains a viable one. If positions like that of Hick's are viable, then it is simply not the case that traditional belief in God is inconsistent with the existence of evil and suffering. We simply do not understand—or, we understand only enough to see that God's purpose is *there* despite evil, although it escapes our full grasp.

---

18. John Hick, *Philosophy of Religion* (Englewood Cliffs, New Jersey: Prentice-Hall, Inc., 1964), 45. For a more detailed presentation, see his *Evil and the God of Love* (New York: Harper & Row, 1966).

THINKING GOD

However, up to this point we have been considering the perspective of logical consistency/inconsistency, of "believing *that*," in the terminology I have been using. To that extent, there is no "actual *formal* or *logical* contradiction between the essential tenets of theism and the reality of evil . . . the problem of evil versus God cannot be decided on purely rational, deductive, or scientific grounds but is, for the atheist no less than for the theist, bound up with a general way of reading the world, a total confrontation, interpretation, and feeling for the whole of things."[19] Again, in the terminology adopted in this chapter, we must consider this issue from the perspective of "believing *in*" God. This is important, because if matters are left where they are, one will have avoided logical inconsistency in one's theistic beliefs by claiming that evil is a mystery; and yet arguably have come no closer to facing the real problem of evil in all its chaotic reality.

The best way to see how the issue of belief *in* God comes into play, in connection with the "mystery" of evil, is to recognize that it has already been playing a role in the discussion. Looking back at the other possible responses to the problem of evil and belief in God, one might well have avoided logical inconsistency by denying God's omnipotence, his goodness, or even the full reality of evil. So why were these options rejected? Essentially, it would seem that people of religious faith did not want to compromise on these points simply because they represented values which were "non-negotiable." Believing in God's absolute power and goodness were values in which people invested, so to speak, and without which, belief in God would not be worth the trouble. Be this as it may, however, to refuse a compromise on the divine attributes is not simply to make a logical/rational point. It is to insist on an intuition about what matters most to us as believers. The reason why this is an important point to bear in mind, is that it allows a dimension into the discussion of evil that speaks to our deepest

---

19. Ed. L. Miller, *God and Reason: An Invitation to Philosophical Theology* (Englewood Cliffs, New Jersey: Prentice-Hall, Inc., 1995), 185.

intuitions about what is valuable in life. When we speak about *believing in* God, as opposed to *believing that* God is x, y, z, etc., we speak about God as a worthy object of devotion, not to be watered down even by the experience of evil and suffering.

Another way to express this point is to ask about the contrary possibility. Supposing that evil was *not* a mystery, and that we could arrive at some kind of a "solution" or adequate response to the problem of evil, given traditional belief in God. What would such a response be like? Having listened to such a response, would we breathe a sigh of relief, and admit that "now we understand"? And if so, would "understanding" alleviate the suffering? Indeed, if we are honest it would seem that the only adequate response to the problem of evil and suffering is to make it go away! By claiming that the problem of evil and suffering, vis-a-vis belief in God, is a mystery, we are essentially refusing any "solutions" as fake. But there is still more to it than that. Unless evil and human suffering are to have the last word—which they threaten to do ultimately through death—it cannot be *only* that we are refusing any viable solution. It must be that we are holding out for a real solution. And according to what we are saying here, the real solution for which we are waiting must be the eradication of evil and suffering, or the making of all things which are, into the way that they ought to be. Since no such eradication appears to take place in this world, does this mean that we are holding out for another world?

It is at this point in the discussion that philosophical reflection runs into a barrier. Many people do indeed *hope* that there is an afterlife, in which evil will exist no more. But how can purely rational reflection hope to talk about this possibility? Are we not at the limits of what we can know?

Whether and to what extent the afterlife can be known is a topic for a later chapter. But this much can be said in regard to the central problem of this chapter. The existence of evil and suffering do pose a real challenge for belief in God. This does not mean that they render our belief *that* God exists as we believe him to, inconsistent. Rather do they challenge our belief *in* God and our existential commitment to him as the locus and source of all that is valuable in human life. Arguably, the manifest existence of evil, together with an ongoing belief in God as all-powerful and all-good, can only be reconciled when some kind of belief in the afterlife is brought in. This is to mix philosophy with the realms of theology and religion, but it would seem that this cannot be avoided. Philosophy shows itself as growing from the same roots in human experience that nourish religion and theology.[20]

---

20. For an interesting discussion of some blind-spots in standard philosophical discussions of evil and belief in God, see Marilyn McCord Adams, *Horrendous Evils and the Goodness of God* (New York: Cornell University Press, 1999). The book tends to show the implausibility of rigidly separating philosophical reflection from religious belief and practice, and examines what contributions an explicitly Christian world-view can make to the discussion.

# 6

## What about Indifference to Religion?

> Nothing I had been taught in my religious education seemed adequate to encompass the grandeur and mystery of what I had learned in science.
>
> —Chet Raymo.[1]

THESE OPENING words from scientist Chet Raymo are so sad. He had been brought up as a Catholic, had received a normal Catholic religious education, and yet that religious education did not open up for him the grandeur and mystery of his scientific education. That is sad because if any curricular discipline should open up grandeur and mystery, it should be religious or theological education. For Raymo, and one suspects for many others, religious education did not prove to be as exciting and as mystagogical as education in the other disciplines and subjects. That could easily lead to a dismissal of religious studies or theology as redundant or even irrelevant. It is this irrelevance of religion or indifference to religion that is the focus of this chapter.

---

1. Chet Raymo, *Skeptics and True Believers: The Exhilarating Connection Between Science and Religion* (New York: MJF Books, 1998), 8.

# THINKING GOD

## THINKING ABOUT SPIRITUAL INDIFFERENCE

It seems clear that there is a distinction to be made between indifference to religion and spiritual indifference. Many people claim to be spiritual but not religious. In this chapter, however, for the sake of brevity both forms will be regarded as pretty much the same. It would be interesting to make comparison in our present day situation to the situations of past generations in the Christian faith. It would be interesting not least because one suspects that "spiritual indifference" in some degree or another is a characteristic of every generation. It would be sheerly romantic to think that any particular historical period is entirely free of challenge in this regard. There was certainly a measure of spiritual indifference at the time of Jesus, and we see it reflected in his teaching. Think of the parable of the sower, for example. The seed that was sown did not everywhere bear fruit. There are no golden ages in the history of the church, ages free of problem and challenge. Having recognized that fact, the burden of this particular chapter is to look at some of the factors that make for spiritual or religious indifference in our time.

The first factor is letting time slip past without adequate reflection on the meaning of life. Constantly people acknowledge or complain that the time of their lives is flashing past with great rapidity. It is not only the case that time slips past, but it is also the case that we are in some degree morally responsible for letting it slip past. Contemporary life is busy, with many responsibilities and duties to be met, and with many challenges and difficulties to be faced. There is only so much time in the day and only so much energy in the person, and it is all too easy to let the time of our lives slip past. When critical issues come to our awareness now and again, they often represent an opportunity for deeper reflection and a sense of direction in life. All too often, however, such opportunities are very short-lived. One author writes: "We bury our occasional intimations of mortality under what Wordsworth called 'the lethargy of custom,' that vast collection of illusions and diversions we refer to as our lives."[2] Describing our lives as "vast collections of illusions and diversions" may seem unduly harsh, but in our better moments most people will recognize some element of truth here.

A second factor has to do with consumerism, one of the essential hallmarks of contemporary Western capitalism. Consumerism is the point of view that maintains that who you are is what you own, and the more you own the more you are. The value of the person is to be measured in terms of their possessions, and what they possess is dependent on income and buying power. In respect of this factor too, it is less the case that people set out to endorse a deliberately consumerist philosophy of life. Just as they let the time of their lives slip past without deliberately doing so, they drift into consumerism without fully intending it. The popular theologian Ronald Rolheiser describes this consumerism very well in these words: "The unconscious, and in many cases the conscious, mythology that moves people today is that of success, of moving up the ladder, of being rich, of having a beautiful body, of being well dressed, of having prestige, of luxuriating in material comfort, of achieving optimally, but in comfort, everything that is potentially attainable with our limits."[3] Who doesn't want to be successful? Or achieve a degree of genuine comfort? Or be acknowledged for competence and expertise by moving up the ladder? These are all very reasonable and, indeed, very good aspirations. The problem lies not in the aspirations but in their ability to anesthetize us to seeking after wisdom through constant habits of reflectiveness.

Beneath this anesthetizing influence lies the massive complex and apparatus of advertising. Since at least the 1960s there has been a growing awareness of the influence of advertising, not

2. David Dawson, "Why are We So Indifferent About Our Spiritual Lives?," in *Why Are We Here?*, ed. Ronald F. Thiemann and William C. Placher, (Harrisburg, PA: Trinity Press International, 1998), 19.

3. Ronald Rohlheiser, O.M.I., *The Shattered Lantern*, rev. ed. (New York: Crossroad, 2001), 31.

least the sheer amount of money that is poured into it. A halt has been called to particular forms of advertising that have a negative impact on people. Nevertheless, the juggernaut of advertising goes on relentlessly. Needless to say, it is not all bad. There is, however, an injurious side to it, well expressed in these words of Archbishop Rowan Williams: "Anything but innocuous is the character of style wars: it is still mercifully rare to murder for a pair of trainers, or to commit suicide because of an inability to keep up with peer group fashion; but what can we say about a marketing culture that so openly feeds and colludes with obsession? What picture of the acting or choosing self is being promoted?"[4] In so many ways the advertising apparatus diminishes human freedom by creating obsession with fashion, entertainment, and even with healthcare. The result is obvious—humans become much less critically reflective. Reduced critical reflectiveness becomes especially acute in the halls of education. School and college are too often seen and appreciated not so much for intellectual and moral development, but as conduits through which to market oneself successfully and so become a money-making machine.

Added to this pervasive consumerism, and perhaps a consequence of it is an intellectual and moral relativism. Ironically, this relativism is seldom chosen. Rather, it is picked up from popular culture, insisting that there is no truth to be known, or more frequently truths are only opinions. One may point out that from a logical point of view the notion that all truths are relative seems to exempt that particular truth, but logic is seldom successful in this area in winning people over.

Finally, there is the centrality of entertainment in our culture. The marvelous advances in technology have made it possible to be entertained anywhere and anytime. There is now an expectation of amusement and entertainment in almost every aspect of life at the flick of a switch or button. This leads immediately to a devaluing

---

4. Rowan D. Williams, "Childhood and Choice," in *Lost Icons, Reflections on Cultural Bereavement* (Edinburgh: T. & T. Clark, 2000), 23.

of critical thinking and reflection, because such thinking can only be done with patience, through genuine inquisitiveness, in silence and solitude, and with a certain humility.

## THE CONSEQUENCE FOR MANY

As a result of these cultural factors many appear to experience a feeling of lostness in western culture. They seem to lack a sense of purpose in life, a *telos* for life as a whole. "Drifting" is the image that comes to mind, drifting from one immediate project to another without a strong inner sense of direction. Optimally, drifting from one specific practical or pleasurable activity to another may yield a high degree of transient satisfaction. The satisfaction is seldom long-lasting. It yields place to further and greater directionless drifting. As a result, depression sets in. Not depression as clinically defined, but a sense that in all of this living-through-drifting something is missing. There develops a pervasive sadness and discontent, a listlessness of spirit, a sadness that quite literally is life-robbing. It is a sadness that has been well described by theologian Frederick Bauerschmidt in these words: "I suspect that it is fundamentally mistaken to see the widespread depression of our times simply as a problem of external circumstances, as if what we need is to find a way to fix things—in our world, in our personal lives—and then we could be happy and contented again. I suspect this is a mistaken view because depression is not so much a matter of being overwhelmed by this or that situation in life, rather it is a matter of being overwhelmed by the very task of being a self."[5] Bauerschmidt is not describing a formally clinical situation, but this overwhelming feeling of not being able to find oneself, so to speak, so as to establish meaning and direction and purpose in life that is long-lasting and more permanently satisfactory.

---

5. Frederick Bauerschmidt, *Mystics Matter Now* (Notre Dame, IN: Sorin Books, 2003), 116–17.

THINKING GOD

## THINKING ALONG WITH HARVEY COX

The retired Harvard theology professor, Harvey Cox, has recently written a book with the intriguing title *The Future of Faith*.[6] Some of Cox's reflections are closely related to our topic. He asks the question: "What does the future hold for religion, and for Christianity in particular?" As he develops his response, he takes a historical perspective and views the history of Christianity as consisting of three periods: the age of faith, the age of belief, and the age of Spirit.

The age of faith began with Jesus and his immediate followers, a period of explosive spiritual growth, catapulting the Christian community to virtually all parts of the Roman Empire. It was not long-lasting, and rapidly developed into the age of belief. This began in the early church when church leaders started to formulate catechetical programs for new recruits who had no personal experience of Jesus and the apostolic community. Out of these catechetical programs gradually came the development of lists of beliefs or creeds, along with the clerical caste. The Emperor Constantine took this stage forward when he passed the Edict of Toleration and began to favor Christianity and its institutions. These policies were further confirmed by the Emperor Theodosius who made Christianity the official religion of the Roman Empire. Cox comments: "For Christianity it proved to be a disaster: its enthronement actually degraded it. From an energetic movement of faith it coagulated into a phalanx of required beliefs, thereby laying the foundation for every succeeding Christian fundamentalism for centuries to come . . . Christianity, at least in its official version, froze into a system of mandatory precepts that were codified into creeds and strictly monitored by a powerful hierarchy and imperial decrees. Heresy became treason, and treason became heresy."[7] This is very strong language and, of course, scholars can with ease show how obviously it is flawed. For example, epistemologically

---

6. Harvey Cox, *The Future of Faith* (New York: HarperCollins, 2009).
7. Ibid., 6.

there can be no faith without some minimal content, and that content is "belief." The development of hierarchy and imperial decrees regulating and governing what Christians "must" believe is true as far as it goes. However, it leaves out the central fact that doctrinal decrees emerged in synods or councils, after rigorous debate and heated exchange, and even then in Newman's conviction at least took one hundred years to be received. Nonetheless, there is something to Cox's analysis. Faith, as our native orientation to the ultimate or the divine, in a sense became secondary to the fund of beliefs, the doctrines and rituals that marked the church. Faith thus understood cannot remain strong and vigorous. There is an obvious disconnect between the religious subject with all the particularities of her experience and understanding and the doctrinal, moral, and liturgical tradition of the church. If one is unable to access intelligently and experientially this tradition in a persuasive fashion and in a way that enriches one's daily living, there is no good compelling reason to stay with the tradition of the church. The age of belief, according to Cox, lasted about 1500 years. It began to ebb with the Enlightenment, the French Revolution, the secularization of Europe, and the anticolonial upheavals of the twentieth century. Cox does not see this long age of belief as simply a dark age. People continued to live by faith and according to the Spirit. Confidence in Christ was the primary orientation of most people, although he thinks that "most people accepted the official belief codes of the church, albeit without much thought."

The age of the Spirit is our present age in the history of Christianity. This new chapter sees Christianity growing faster than ever before, but outside the geographical, political, and in some ways intellectual confines of the West. The emphases in the age of the Spirit are upon spiritual experience, discipleship, and hope, and attention to creeds is much less important, as are hierarchies. The age of the Spirit is the beginning of the post-Constantinian era. The growth in the numbers of people who are self-described as "spiritual" but not "religious" is another indicator of the age of the Spirit. Many people seem drawn to the experiential rather than to the doctrinal elements of religion. In Cox's words, "The experience of the divine is displacing theories about it."[8] Alternatively expressed, subjective faith is primary, not objective or ecclesial belief. "Christianity understood as a system of beliefs guarded and transmitted through a privileged religious institution by a clerical class is dying. Instead, today Christianity as a way of life shared in a vast variety of ways by a diverse global network of fellowships is arising."[9]

## THREE COMMENTS ON THE INSTITUTIONAL CHURCH

If we are not to write the obituary for the church and institutional Christianity, and such obituaries have many failed precedents in the past and usually when scientism is in the ascendant, some positive response needs to be made. Three points immediately suggest themselves. First, one needs to acknowledge that institutions, including belief systems, often do get in the way of human flourishing, not through human malice so much as basic human ineptitude and complacency. Institutions very easily can give the impression that "man was made for the Sabbath, not the Sabbath for man." This is true of all institutions—think of local government, think of educational institutions, think, really, of any institution. The philosopher Michael Novak writes: "Every social institution is a clumsy thing."[10] Novak is stating the obvious but the obvious needs to be stated.

Second, any reasonable human being will recognize that the mediocrity of the church is no less obvious than one's own mediocrity. If I fail to recognize and accept my own intellectual and moral

8. Ibid., 20.
9. Ibid., 196.
10. Michael Novak and Jana Novak, *Tell Me Why* (New York and London: Pocket Books, 1998), 16.

and relational mediocrity, then I am failing as a human being. If, in fact, I do recognize it, then the mediocrity of the institutional church falls into place. It's not just "them," it's me. While I am persuaded that this line of thinking is helpful, its persuasiveness is diminished by such things as the widespread report on sexual abuse and consequent cover-up, by what appears to be at times an arbitrary use of power and authority that tends to run roughshod over the living experience of people. Of course, there is no golden age in the history of the church. Every age has its own problems and challenges, contributions and flaws. However, in various parts of the West at least, we seem to have reached a point of real crisis in respect of the credibility of many church authorities.

Third, one's vision is always fragmentary and conditioned. There is more to the institutional church than what we see. Necessarily, we frame both individuals and institutions in terms of what we are able to see, in terms of what we want to see. However, there is always more to see than meets my particular eye. One ought to notice the negative aspects of the institutional church. Not to do so would be to fail as an intelligent human being. Beyond that, however, it needs to be said that much good is done in and through the institutional church, especially through the millions of ordinary, anonymous Christians. If I failed to recognize that, then the failure is my failure really to see what is there.

Nonetheless, the question still needs to be faced, "Why is institutional religion so unattractive to so many in our time?" Impossible to answer in a total way, but at least we may posit some impressionistic ideas.[11] First, and very basically, people want to choose their existential identity in life rather than having it handed to them on a plate by their families or by their living contexts. It is a matter of wanting to shape one's self rather than

11. I am following here some of the considerations of Rowan Williams, the current Archbishop of Canterbury, in a lecture entitled "The Spiritual and the Religious: Is the Territory Changing?" Delivered in Westminster Cathedral, London, on April 17, 2008. The text of the lecture is available from the Archbishop of Canterbury's website.

letting oneself be shaped entirely by one's environment. In other words, one might say that the institutional apparatus of support for religious practice has largely fallen away. The North African patristic author, Tertullian, once said: "Christians are made not born." People want to make themselves what they want to make themselves. They do not wish to be something simply because of the circumstances of birth.

For many, institutional religious allegiance is making over some aspect of oneself to others in ways that seem to compromise both one's freedom and integrity. It is about subjecting oneself to patterns of ritual and codes of behavior and beliefs that do not seem to integrate well with one's growing sense of identity and appropriate autonomy. The spiritual on the other hand opens up personal perspectives for flourishing that appear to be much broader than the institutional allows, and that are freely chosen by the person.

Second, association with an institutional religious faith is often seen as aligning oneself to some kind of exclusivism when it comes to truth, insight, and wisdom. If one is committed to a specific faith, one seems necessarily to be committed to a refusal to recognize the values in other traditions of faith. Many contemporaries experience a widespread resistance to any kind of perceived monopolistic claims when it comes to religious truth. As Archbishop Rowan Williams puts it, "If we are looking for spiritual resources in our modern environment, they have to be inclusive and generative of liberty." Spiritual resources that are judged to be exclusivist are deemed to be irrelevant, and thus unworthy of both exploration and personal commitment. It is not so much the case that people no longer ask fundamental questions about the ultimate meaning of life. It is more the case that they wish to be determinative of their own answers to these questions, vis-à-vis a wide range of traditions including religious traditions, rather than to subscribe to answers that they are given in a particular tradition that sees itself as absolute and supreme.

*What about Indifference to Religion?*

An apologist for Christianity might say by way of response that Christian faith is participation in a comprehensive way of life, a comprehensive vision of all reality and one's place in it. It is not in the first place simply assent to a system of beliefs, a code of moral values, and a pattern of worship. Within this comprehensive vision and way of life there is room for individual maneuver. Christians are united in essentials, but that unity is not the same as absolute uniformity. Fair enough! If the apologist's answer has some measure of credibility, the question still remains, "Why is Christianity not seen like that?" Why is it that for so many, being a Christian actively is seen as joining a religious club in which one is expected to believe the beliefs, to live by the moral code, and to worship in a particular way? Why is it that Christianity is often perceived as opposed to individual initiative and to individual responsibility-taking? It may be due to such factors as widespread theological illiteracy, inadequate catechesis at all stages of life, and poor preaching. If some of these things were attended to, perhaps, Christianity would not be seen as a rigid and dogmatic system and set of institutions. It might be seen as more invitational and participatory from the vantage point of the subject. Thus, for example, the Dominican theologian Fergus Kerr has written: "The Roman Catholic Church is not the monolithic entity that her enemies and her most zealous members believe. Beliefs are not held univocally, or with clarity, or across the board."[12]

## A WAY FORWARD FOR THEOLOGIANS AND LEADERS IN THE CHURCH

There is no panacea. There is no perfect pastoral formula, the application of which will turn things around so that people would become more genuinely reflective, more philosophically and theo-

---

12. Fergus Kerr, OP, *Twentieth Century Catholic Theologians* (Oxford: Basil Blackwell Publishing, 2007), 203.

logically informed, and better able to make a lifelong commitment as Christians. Perhaps, however, some suggestions might be made to assist theologians and leaders in the church to develop a style of ministry and theological reflection that may make present situations better. Let's look briefly at four suggestions.[13]

1. Be more experience-based in theology. Theology, of course, is a multi-disciplinary field ranging over all manner of things requiring a variety of skills: methodologies for understanding Scripture and the biblical languages; church history; systematic theology; pastoral theology; canon law; liturgy, and so forth. There is no suggestion that these disciplines and their methodologies should be dumbed down. But the professionals who do theology in a formal way, as it were, and who have degrees in theology, should also acknowledge that God is at work in the experience and lives of ordinary people. A more experience-based theology is "a theology with a greater awareness of and trust in the action of God's spirit in the lives of people." More is going on theologically in the lives of ordinary people than might pass muster from a formally theological point of view.

2. Be more pastoral. If the first recommendation is taken to heart, then theology must become more pastoral. Theology is not about abstractions, but about living relationships, human and divine. Attending to such relationships with great care and sensitivity will demand deep and richly founded skills of pastoral theological reflection.

3. Be ready to take risks. Responsible risk taking will demand of ecclesial leaders and theologians; in the words of Kevin Kelly, "A theology which is prepared to think creatively and imaginatively, rather than be held back by an over-cautious fear of possible consequences . . ." The circumstances of people's lives

---

13. These reflect in part the thinking of moral theologian Kevin T. Kelly, "Confessions of an Ageing Moral Theologian," *The Furrow* (February, 2004), 82–91.

are so varied and different. A creative and imaginative approach to theology is not necessarily "doing your own thing" without due regard for the church's tradition, without regard for the Magisterium. Rather, it is a way of doing theology that recognizes as fundamental that theology is for people, not people for theology. It is a style of reflection and action that is more tolerant of diversity. I often think of church history as the real theology of liberation because it demonstrates so lucidly that the Catholic tradition is much more pluriform than some would have us believe. There are diverse ways of thinking theologically about the same Christian faith. St. Thomas Aquinas thought differently from St. Bonaventure, the former more Aristotelian, the latter more Platonic. Some like to read Balthasar, some Rahner. There is no revealed philosophy or metaphysics. Responsible risk taking is aware of these factors.

4. Be more open to ambiguity. Few important things in life are absolutely clear, but have a necessary element of ambiguity about them. This recognition helps us practice, again in the words of Kevin Kelly looking back on a lifetime of reflection and pastoral ministry, "a theology more prepared to accept *en route* pastoral solutions despite their being tinged by compromise and ambiguity."

It is impossible to think of the widespread indifference to religious faith and practice disappearing anytime soon. The reflections offered in this inchoate chapter indicate that substantive improvement in our present ecclesial circumstances will largely be dzependent upon human relationships. Ecclesial relationships that are respectful and inviting, that are challenging and courteous, that are informed by deeply appropriated and personalized theological convictions, will be essential.

# 7

# Is There Life After Death?

> *Before this terrible mystery of mortality, face to face with the Sphinx, man adopts a variety of attitudes and seeks variously to console himself for having been born.*
>
> —Miguel de Unamuno

THE ABOVE lines were penned by Miguel de Unamuno in a work dealing exclusively with death and the longing for immortality. They are somber words, but oddly suited to the aims of this chapter. In a previous chapter on the problem of evil and suffering, it was concluded that there can be no complete solution to this problem, unless we accept some version of consummation in God. Since this is supposed to happen beyond the experience of this life, the topic of life after death was effectively introduced already. Yet, precisely because it was introduced in connection with evil and suffering, it might be thought that the question of eternal life is only relevant in an indirect way. That is, if we did not suffer to the extent that we do, we would have no need of it. But this is only one side of the story. If we did not feel, whilst suffering/experiencing evil, that something had been lost to us, then any longing to have things put right in the next life would be hard to understand. It is because there is a kind of *reflection* of the afterlife (which is communion with God) in our experience, that suffering beings feel robbed. Hence the longing for heaven/consummation in God has a deeper root than our experience of evil and suffering—evil and suffering simply alert us to the fact that there is a goodness and sweetness to life, which cannot now be fully recovered—but which we feel should eventually be restored (even if the latter is beyond our human powers).

If we were to stop here, then we are left with a fairly concise, if simplified, version of what believing Christians hold about the connection between this life and the next. Now, while it might be granted by many religious people, and perhaps even by those professing no religious faith, that the *idea* of heaven, or an afterlife where everything is "put right" is an attractive one, the crucial question is whether it is a reality or not. "If wishes were horses, beggars would ride," is an oft-quoted adage, which captures this sentiment. Maybe it is true at some level that everyone would like to believe in some such idea of life after death where all wrongs/sufferings are redressed—but is it intellectually honest or respectable to do so? A plethora of problems arise in connection with the belief in life after death, not all of which can be examined here. In what follows, three closely related types of question will be examined, and a response suggested. In brief, it will be asked: (i) What does life after death *mean*? (ii) Why is it considered *important*? (iii) Can there be any good *arguments*/convincing *evidence* for it? I do not claim that by the end of this chapter the difficulties and ambiguities with belief in life after death will have gone away. However, I will argue that this belief is coherent and important to human life. Furthermore, after noting some of the evidence and arguments typically presented for this belief, an attempt will be made to understand why they are/are not considered persuasive.

# THINKING GOD

## I

(i) There seems to be an initial difficulty in raising the issue of life after death, and which should be looked at first. Put quite simply, if one has really *died*, then it is nonsense to speak of a life after death. On the other hand, if there really *is* life beyond the grave, then in what sense can a person really have died at all? As one philosopher put it, "If it is the case that in order to think survival of bodily death, one has got to think bodily death away, then what one is thinking is not survival but simply the absence of the condition one is supposed to survive."[1] The advantage of stating the problem in this way is that it forces one to clarify one's belief from the outset. For obviously, if we are to speak of life after death, then there must be some form of *continuity*, such that the "I" that I am in this world is "the same" "I" after death—otherwise, whatever else might be said, "It will not be *me* that has survived, if anything has at all!" And herein lays the difficulty. For it seems to be an empirical fact that our bodies decompose, and hence do not survive. Thinking clearly and coherently about life after death then, demands that we take this fact squarely into account. So, what could it mean to say that "I survive death," in a Christian context? What kind of continuity would there be between the "I before death," and the "I after death"? Typically, there have been two main answers to this problem, and hence two ways of understanding the "continuity of the I." One tends to emphasize the "resurrection of the body"; the other tends to speak of the "immortality of the soul/mind." We will look at each in turn before offering a response of our own.

(ii) Christianity has traditionally spoken of the resurrection of the *body*. And many people have interpreted this resurrection, and hence the nature of death, along biological lines. In regard to death, if one takes a standard biological account, there is a gradual breakdown of the overall functioning of a living organism.

---

1. Anthony Flew, "Death," in *New Essays in Philosophical Theology*, ed. A. Flew & A. MacIntyre (New York: Macmillan Company, 1968), 262.

Eventually, it reaches a point where the organism can no longer maintain itself—major organs fail, etc.—and biological corruption/decomposition sets in. This is a fairly straightforward description of bodily death. Therefore, to speak of the resurrection of the body would be to think on the same biological plane. Christians are to expect that, when Christ comes again, the biological *dis-integration* will be reversed, and we will be *re-integrated* in Christ. That it has not happened yet, it would be said, (and as empirical observation would attest) simply shows that we are still waiting for Christ. One difficulty with this view of what "resurrection of the body" could mean is that, apparently, one would have "disappeared," or gone out of existence during the interim period between one's death and resurrection. It might of course be said that this is no problem at all, since one would find oneself alive again in the end. Yet, this is precisely the point—the person who "finds himself" alive again—on what grounds are they the *same* person, and not simply an ingenious replica complete with memories, looks, and personality? To get around this problem, some philosophers have held what might be called the "temporary disembodiment" theory. Basically, one's non-physical soul would survive the original bodily death; would guarantee continuity of personal identity in the interim period; and then be reunited with one's own body in the final resurrection. Indeed, this theory "entails that human souls can animate both normal earthly bodies and glorified resurrection bodies. Continuity between the two bodies is provided by the presence of both the same soul and the same matter in both bodies."[2] This, in fact, was the position of Thomas Aquinas.[3] It represents in many ways a "compromise position" between the view of immortality as

2. Stephen Davis, "Traditional Christian Belief in the Resurrection of the Body," in *Philosophy and Death*, ed. S. Brennan and R. Stainton (Toronto: Broadview Press, 2010), 83. Originally published in *New Scholasticism* 62: 72–97.

3. For an illuminating discussion of Aquinas' precise views on this question, see Mary F. Rousseau, "Elements of a Thomistic Philosophy of Death," *The Thomist*, vol. 43, no. 4, (October, 1979).

the continuance of the rational soul (which we will look at next); and of the resurrection of the physical body.

However, some philosophers have explored other possibilities for the meaning of bodily resurrection—presumably because they find it difficult to accept that the very same body, rotting in the ground/cremated and scattered, will be raised up again in each identical particle. Why not postulate that at the resurrection, an "exact replica" of oneself as a psycho-physical entity, will be recreated, and in a different space dimension from the one we now inhabit? John Hick, through a series of thought-experiments and hypothetical scenarios, asks us whether it is really so very implausible. If it turns out to be at least a logical possibility; and if we would naturally recognize a replica as somehow "the same self"; then we would be permitted "to preserve a personal identity which we are supposing to be wholly bound up with the body,"[4] but without the seeming absurdities and difficulties that attend a more "literal" view.[5] Hick freely admits that this all stays at the level of logical possibility—not at the level of fact. One has the impression that this is where Christian faith would step in for him, such that his philosophizing serves to show that what the faith holds is not impossible or contradictory. At any rate, both the replica theory as well as the more traditional theory of temporary disembodiment attempt to hold onto a view of life after death which stresses the body. At an intuitive level, many people feel that this is more in touch with the nature of human beings—despite a strong "Platonic" view to the contrary, humans are held to be inextricably tied to their bodies.

4. John Hick, *Death and Eternal Life* (Louisville: John Knox Press, 1994), 296.

5. Davis, [*op. cit.*] gives a resume of some of the more common accusations: "What if a Christian dies at sea and his body is eaten by various fishes who then scatter to the seven seas? . . . Or what if another Christian is eaten by cannibals, so that the material of her body becomes the material of their bodies? . . . Who gets what particles? How does God decide?" p. 89. Davis points out that the standard response is often to appeal to God's omnipotence, in properly reconstituting people.

(iii) But the bodily perspective has a competitor. If the bodily notion of life after death can be termed the viewpoint of St. Paul,[6] then it can be counterposed to the Greek, Platonic conception, which tends to view life after death as a purely spiritual/mental "mind" or "spirit," which therefore can be said to survive death.[7] Elements of this approach seem to carry over into the thought of some Christian writers such as Augustine.[8] People who think in this way about life after death are providing their own answer to the initial question that was posed—namely, how we are to think of "the continuity of the I." In this case, advocates of "the immortality of the soul" believe that it is our rational soul that lends us our identity, even in this life. Thus, in the afterlife it is nothing like a *loss* to have this rational soul as the only thing remaining. Indeed, Plato spoke of it as a kind of liberation. Nevertheless, if one is to hold this view of life after death, then some clarification is in order, since a "disembodied" existence is difficult to imagine. One philosopher asks, "How, for example, are experiences or thought possible without a body? How, in the absence of limbs and organs, could we be said to act? How without any physical way of connecting our ideas and intentions to the world, or to others, could we change things in the world or communicate?"[9] Just as in the case of John Hick's thought-experiments on physical replicas, it is possible to do the same with trying to imagine a purely non-physical/mental post-mortem existence. H.H. Price attempted something

---

6. Although St. Paul tends to speak of "spiritual bodies," See, *God and Reason*, ed. L. Miller (Englewood Cliffs, New Jersey: Prentice-Hall Inc., 1995), 187–90.

7. The classical discussion of these issues by Plato is contained in his dialogue, *The Phaedo*. As for his basic position on what "death" is, Plato says "The body comes to be separated by itself apart from the soul, and the soul comes to be separated by itself apart from the body . . . is death anything else than that?"

8. In his dialogue, *The Soliloquies*, Augustine has a proof for immortality from the mind's knowledge of truth.

9. Anthony O'Hear, *Philosophy in the New Century* (London: Continuum, 2003), 183.

like this, suggesting that "the Next World, if there is one, might be a world of mental images . . . to those who experience it an image-world would be just as 'real' as this present world is; and perhaps so like it, that they would have considerable difficulty in realizing that they were dead."[10] Perhaps what Price means is that beyond the mental *appearance* of the real, what could we mean when we talk about "the real"? Common sense often assumes that there is a "real world" beyond/behind our mental images and our subjective experiences. But even if that were true, the only reality *we* know and have access to is the one that *appears to us*. If the realm of appearances is running smoothly, then it is hard to imagine any problems arising from "the real world" behind those appearances.[11] In any case, we can imagine such an existence, a world with images so vivid that the question of "the real" becomes superfluous. Price concludes "My point is only that it is not absurd; or, if you like, that it is at any rate intelligible."[12]

(iv) At this point in the discussion, a minimal clarification of what life after death could mean has been developed—there must be some sort of continuity between the "I" of this world and the "I" which continues in the next. Having said that, the two main competitors for how this continuity is to be understood—the mental/non-physical soul theory and the physical body theory (or even some combination of them both, as in "temporary disembodiment")—show themselves as attempts to shed some light on what this continuity of identity means. The difficulties raised here are omnipresent throughout the Christian tradition. On the one

---

10. Reprinted in *Philosophy of Religion*, 4th Edition, ed. Peterson, Hasker, Reichenback and Basinger (New York: Oxford University Press, 2010), 466–67. Originally delivered as the Sarum Lectures, in 1971.

11. A number of popular films have explored some of the complicated issues involved here. For instance, *The Matrix* and *The Truman Show* do a particularly good job of bringing some of the difficulties to light. At a more philosophical level, this position is known normally as "idealism." Well known representatives include George Berkeley and G. W. F. Hegel.

12. Ibid., 472.

hand there is a belief in life after death. On the other hand there is an attempt to clarify what that could mean. Yet, both the physical and non-physical approaches seem to be *logically possible* explanations, so which one should be accepted? Indeed, does a failure to select one of them, due to an apparent lack of conclusive evidence/reasoning, suggest that our belief in life after death is itself groundless, without any convincing foundation in reality? At least some critics of traditional religion have argued this.

At this point I would like to offer a suggestion for coming to grips with what could be meant by life beyond death, at least in regard to the most basic contours of the problem. There are two central points to be noted. Firstly, in discussions of what life after death could mean, it is the notion of *self* that is central, *not* the notion of a "body" or the notion of a "mind" (or even some combination of the two). The human self, or person, is at the center of the issue. This may seem to be ignoring the difficult questions of what we are actually to understand by a "self." But this brings us to the second point. For it is imperative to distinguish between two levels of meaning and discourse. There is what we might call the everyday, conversational, pre-reflective level of meaning, where concepts like "self," "person," and even "death" are talked about, sometimes as though there were no peculiarities or ambiguities about them. And then there is the reflective level of discourse, which is the one familiar to scientists, philosophers, and theologians. Now, what I would like to claim is that, in this particular case, debates about bodies and souls, physical and mental, biological and spiritual are *secondary* to our primary familiarity with what "self" means. It is because we *first* have a rough, intuitive notion of self that we can go on to ask ourselves questions like, "Is it only something physical?" or "Is there a spiritual self which survives bodily death?" While no lasting agreement might be reached over these secondary, reflective questions, we should at least not lose sight of the primary level of discourse, which allowed us to ask these questions in the first place.

The advantage, I believe, of looking at the matter in this fashion, is that we need not get bogged down in contentious debates about the *details* of life after death, and which out of a number of competing "theories" of it we are to choose. While further questions can always be asked at the reflective level, what was always meant by life after death was that my-self, your-self, our-selves, will not pass out of existence or disappear, despite the phenomenon which we call "death." If it is possible to understand this point, then it is also possible to contextualize further discussions about what the details of this purported self could mean. Thus, upon further reflection, we might feel that this human self cannot only mean something physical (our identities remain in tact if we lose a limb—we don't say that "*we* have been lessened"—except humorously, perhaps). Again, neither do we want to discount our very real physical existence, as though our bodies were entirely negligible extensions of our essential selves. The main point of all this is that a central meaning can be given to the notion of life after death, even if reflection shows that further questions remain unanswered. Earlier it was asked whether a lack of agreement about the reflectively articulated details of the self's post-mortem existence means that this belief should be abandoned as empty. It should be clear that this does not at all follow. The lack of detailed, substantial agreement about what the "self" (at a reflective level) could mean is not an objection to the continued existence of the self after death. In fact, since it seems to be the case that there is no real agreement as to what the "self" could mean *here and now*, then we would have just as much ground to claim that there is no existence of the self *before* death, and who would really claim that?[13] Further

13. Interestingly, if one were to say something like, "the self is an illusion," it could still be explained on the model I am proposing. Buddhists, for instance, admit that there is at least the "appearance" of a self, at what I have been calling the pre-reflective level. The Buddhist has simply gone on to the reflective level, at which he concludes that what was present at the pre-reflective level was an illusion. For our purposes, the salient point is that there is a concept of self present to people at a general, pre-reflective level,

*reflection* about what reflection has concluded about pre-reflective experience should at least raise questions about a position that denies the basic intuitions that gave reflection its start.

## II

In the previous section an attempt was made to clarify the meaning of life after death. What might be called a "minimalist" account was given, not in an attempt to sidestep the details, but rather to highlight what was central to the notion before details were even considered. But the next question that arises is as to the *value* of life after death. Why is the notion of the afterlife such an important feature in Christian belief? That it is so important is clear. As Saint Paul succinctly put it, "If there is no resurrection of the dead . . . your faith has been in vain." It is difficult to answer this question, but perhaps the following could be said. It seems to be the case that in human experience the good things which we have, we want to last. Now, clearly, many of the things that we own will not last, but there is an implicit expectation that if something is "worth anything," it won't immediately break or be taken from us. Yet, there is a higher level of goods than things—namely, interpersonal relationships. The relationships that we build with people, at varying levels, have an expectation of permanence built into them. This is more easily seen in very intimate relationships, such as parents-children, husband-wife, etc. There does appear to be an implicit trust that "what you build together" will continue, even as many of the experiences within the relationship are changing. Thus the devastation wreaked by intimate relationships gone bad. Now, the reason that these examples are given—common enough knowledge though they are—is that death seems to be the ultimate breaking apart of any expectation of permanence. All of the good things that one has in one's experience, from trivial possessions

---

regardless of what further rational reflection leads one to say about it.

to profound human relationships, seem to be cut off at the root. It may be that this is all well-known, but from the perspective I have been developing, death "structurally interferes" with the way in which we experience the goods of this life. As such, if death really is the end of everything good in life, then it is not just a phenomenon waiting for us "at the end of the road"; it is a shadow which seems to haunt our experience of goodness with ultimate doom. In so far as, for instance, a love-relationship is experienced by us as a "lasting thing," death cannot but fail to overshadow and negatively affect the experience. The reason, then, why the afterlife is considered such an important issue, goes arm-in-arm with why we consider the things we love *here and now* important. If you truly love, then you must at least truly hope that it is not all about to irrevocably, permanently end.[14] That is, the importance of the afterlife as an issue is essentially connected with the importance of life-here-and-now as an issue.

That something significant is being recognized here can be seen indirectly by way of a typical type of objection made to the value of belief in life after death. The German philosopher Ludwig Feuerbach gave the clearest articulation of the view that belief in another life, another world beyond this one, was not only illusory, but pernicious. Essentially, belief in God involved man in a kind of "self-alienation," whereby mankind projects what are essentially human characteristics onto a fantastical realm of perfection. To make matters worse (and what is perhaps the root of it) people would then tend to look forward to this future realm of perfection and turn against the things of this world as so much miserable delay. If we were only to rid ourselves of this belief, Feuerbach insists, we would be able to focus on the here and now, and on improving things for ourselves. Thus, "instead of belief in God, belief of man

14. Gabriel Marcel has had a lot to say about the connections between love, hope, and immortality: "To love a being is to say, 'thou, thou shalt not die' . . . the promise of eternity which is enclosed in our love, in our mutual pledge." Gabriel Marcel, *The Mystery of Being*, trans. René Hague, vol. 2, (Chicago: Henry Regnery Company, 1960), 171–73.

in himself; instead of orientation to another world, commitment to the present world, which certainly needs to be changed."[15] The point of Feuerbach's critique, regardless of its ultimate truth, is that the this-world, afterlife connection can turn into a dualism that robs the genuine goods of this world of their value and robs human beings of the desire to improve them where they can. Thus, belief in the afterlife turns out to erode the values of this life.

It appears that Feuerbach's critique is only effective if the afterlife is viewed dualistically, as a reality utterly cut off from the here and now. Dualistically speaking, there would be a tendency to either turn against the world (be "other-worldly" in the bad sense); or turn against the whole conception of an afterlife (which usually accompanies a more general rejection of God). I believe that Feuerbach's view involves a misconception. Only when belief in the afterlife is seen as an "enabling condition" for the goods of this life, is its value properly understood. What has been said up to this point might be viewed as an attempt to bring the afterlife and this life together, as inextricably intertwined. However, there is a danger of going too far. Is there, after all, *no* real difference between the value of the afterlife and the values we experience here and now? An example of the distortion that occurs when the distinction is completely collapsed can be seen in some of the caricatures of the afterlife—we sing in a choir, float around like angels, engage in intellectual contemplation, etc. Images drawn from activities we engage in here and now, and things we imagine here and now, are supposed to adequately characterize our belief in life after death. At an extreme level this view would see the afterlife simply as an indefinite *continuation* of what we experience here and now. Bernard Williams brings up the character of Elina Makropulos, from a play by Karel Čapek. This lady, having drunk an elixir of life, has reached the age of 342 with no prospect of death in sight.

---

15. Hans Küng, *Eternal Life? Life after Death as a Medical, Philosophical, and Theological Problem*, trans. Edward Quinn (New York: Image Books, 1985), 29.

However, instead of being comforted by this situation, she is overcome by a feeling of boredom—life has become joyless precisely through the endless repetition of the good experiences of this life. Williams remarks, "There is no desirable or significant property which life would have more of, or have more unqualifiedly, if we lasted for ever."[16] Thus, the prospect of a continuation of the goods of this life, stretching out into infinity, is itself seen not as a good/value, but rather as something to be feared. Another writer comments that "it is rather the possibility of continuing after death that I find troubling. It is not just that annihilation would be vastly preferable to the torments of the damned so lovingly described by Dante; it is that even painless perpetuity would be appalling."[17]

If, as was originally maintained, we are to understand the afterlife as part of the structure of the here and now—as a kind of built-in expectation of permanence—then everything will turn on how this permanence is viewed. It is important that it is not utterly cut off from the things we love in this world, but it seems equally important that it not be simply an extension of them. So what is it that Christians are indicating through somewhat clumsy metaphors and images of the hereafter? As in the first section I would like to offer a minimalist suggestion for contextualizing this problem. It involves (i) seeing all the values/goods of this life as *participations* in the good of the afterlife, i.e., God; and (ii) seeing the good of the afterlife (God) as *unlimited* in scope. In regard to seeing all goods of this life as participations in the good of the afterlife, what is being said is that there is a dependence on a "horizon of goodness/value," which is not simply the same as all the individual goods and values that we experience here and now. This point can be illustrated from within the realm of worldly goods and values. For instance, a person goes through different stages of their life. Typically, the goods and values which inform experi-

---

16. Bernard Williams, "The Makropulos Case: Reflections on the Tedium of Immortality," in *Philosophy and Death*, 213.

17. Anthony Kenny, *What I Believe* (New York: Continuum, 2006) 164–65.

ence at one stage are not those of a later stage—people "move on." However, both stages are recognized (at least at the time) as being "instances of values/goods." In a person's evolving life and experience there is a "horizon of goodness/value," which may be "filled in" in different ways at different stages—but which, nevertheless, goes beyond, or *transcends,* the many individual goods/values of experience. In as much as we see all our goods/values "participating" in this horizon of goodness/value, we have taken the first step towards understanding how there can be an overarching value (the afterlife), which is somehow both *present* in our everyday loves and values and yet, strangely, always *beyond* them as a kind of horizon. Interestingly, the attempt to be more "precise" about this horizon (as in the remarks by William and Kenny), by "specifying" its nature, would be to confuse the horizon with a particular manifestation of it.

The second point continues where the first left off. Borrowing a phrase from St. Anselm, who sees God as "that than which no greater can be conceived," the value-horizon of the afterlife (which, after all, is consummation in God) must be seen as *beyond any conceivable limitations.* The reason why this is important is that it helps us to see a problem with views of the afterlife that portray it as "boring" or as a rather insipid "painless perpetuity." For it is quite clear, upon our premises, that to say as much about the afterlife is to paint it as something *limited* in its value. If the horizon of goodness in which our values participate, and which is beyond all finite limitations, is portrayed as lacking in goodness, then we can well reply that this is not what we understand by the afterlife/consummation in God. When offered an image/metaphor of what this horizon of goodness will amount to, at least we know enough about the horizon to discount images that go directly against its nature. Ultimately, then, we would be in the position of saying that although we do not know exactly how the afterlife will be, we do know that it will be unlimited in goodness/value. Therefore, any image that tries to portray it as "mixed with some shortcoming" is a *misrepresentation* of it. Furthermore, since our experience of goods/values in this life is always mixed with some form of limitation, it would seem that *no* image of the afterlife will be able to convey its unlimited value/goodness. The upshot of this second section of the value of belief in life *after* death is that we need it in order to hold onto the values of life *before* death. They are not separate realms; their unity involves the participation of this world's values in the value of the next; and we know enough about the value of the life to come to refuse any image of it which limits it to the imperfect experiences of this world's values/goods.

### III

The final question to be faced in this section is whether or not there are any convincing arguments or evidence for life after death. Even if it could be assigned a roughly coherent meaning and shown to be an important issue, could it still all be "wishful thinking"? Two authors mentioned already—Hick and Price—both attempted to show that life after death (whether physical or non-physical) was at least a logical possibility. It would not be absurd or self-contradictory to hold this belief, but would it be true? A large portion of the western philosophical tradition held that it was possible to logically *prove* or *demonstrate* the immortality of the rational soul. Elaborate arguments were set forth in intricate language with the express purpose of forcing one to concede that there was indeed life after death. One belief which many of them seem to have had in common, is that there is something peculiar about thought and thinking-selves, which implies a connection to immortality. This might be a direct connection, for instance, where there is a link between the thinking self and the Truth which it thinks;[18] or an indirect connection, for instance, where the notion of physical death as dis-integration, is found inapplicable to the thinking-self

18. Augustine's approach in *The Soliloquies*.

and its thoughts.[19] I do not wish to rule out these proofs or to claim that they do not work. But one thing has to be admitted—almost nobody today, religious people notwithstanding, feel that these proofs are relevant. Most probably suspect that they do not succeed as proofs either. Why is this?

The most obvious reason is the dominance of the natural sciences. Their general superiority to all other viewpoints is often thought to be obvious. Thus, previous metaphysical worldviews upon which proofs for the immortality of the soul depend are thought to be obsolete, even worthless. Indeed, the emphasis that these types of proof put on thought itself, and on the thinking-self, is entirely unjustified from the perspective of science. Whatever "thought" is, scientists would claim, it is simply one more natural phenomenon alongside all the others. It can be studied in the same way, using the same methods, and it has no more intrinsic importance than any other thing under investigation. With such an emphasis placed on the uniformity of "scientific method," it is not surprising that key distinctions will emerge. The most important of them, for our purposes, is the so-called "fact-value" distinction.

It is important at least to partially understand the distinction commonly made between facts and values because it summarizes much of what passes for common knowledge today. It is captured succinctly by Hilary Putnam who claims that "the idea that 'value judgments are subjective' is a piece of philosophy that has gradually come to be accepted by many people as if it were common sense."[20] Putnam further clarifies this position as holding that "'statements of fact' are capable of being 'objectively true' and capable, as well, of being 'objectively warranted,' while value judgments . . . are incapable of objective truth and objective warrant."[21] In other words, the dominant scientific world-view of today tends to assume a

19. One of Aquinas' arguments in the *Summa Theologiae*.
20. Hilary Putnam, *The Collapse of the Fact/Value Dichotomy, and Other Essays* (Cambridge, MA: Harvard University Press, 2002), 1.
21. Ibid.

distinction between facts and values, and to assume further, that values are not "objective." This means, in effect, that they have no "truth-value," or significance, other than as bio-chemical processes going on within a subject who has the emotions usually attached to such values.

It is interesting to note in this connection, that there grew up as a result of this rigid distinction, an attempt to find "factual grounds" (i.e., "scientific" grounds) for life after death. For example, societies for "psychical research" emerged towards the end of the nineteenth century, with the purpose of investigating any factual evidence for the afterlife.[22] Interviews and experiments were conducted with mediums and psychics, and the results were published in a detached even somewhat skeptical manner. In the twentieth century, a famous book was published by Raymond A. Moody containing the accounts of numerous patients who had been "clinically dead," but who had "come back to life."[23] It was found that there were numerous types of overlap and similarity. Many of them seemed to describe a kind of "post-mortem" existence akin to an ethereal, floating experience, accompanied by a loving presence, and so on. These types of approach have become famous, and although they are certainly ambiguous and far from conclusive, have seemed to point to odd forms of experience that science is not fully able to explain. The significant point for our purpose is that the need was felt to look into the "scientific-factual" grounds instead of trying to come up with new or better forms of rational proof for immortality.

So how do things stand with the problem of life after death, in particular, with the attempt to *prove* such a thing? Obviously,

---

22. One of the most famous and interesting figures associated with the American Society for Psychical Research, was the philosopher and psychologist William James. See the fascinating study by Deborah Blum, *Ghost Hunters: William James and the Search for Scientific Proof of Life After Death* (New York: Penguin Press, 2006).

23. Raymond A. Moody, *Life After Life* (St. Simons Island, GA: Mockingbird Books, 1975).

the belief in the afterlife represents a deeply-held value of much of humanity. But, according to the fact-value distinction, this belief, together with the reasoning involved in "proving" it, must be treated as just one more fact amidst a world of facts. In other words, even if it is true that most people *want* to live forever, this is not essentially different from the general biological urge for survival that we can observe throughout nature. Perhaps the only difference is that the human urge to live forever is essentially tied to intellect/reason, which would explain the drive to "prove" it rationally. But, scientifically speaking, there is nothing about the peculiarly human *intellectual* drive to survive that would serve to set it off from other biological species. That human reason, beyond simply devising weapons and tools for survival, should go on to consider abstract proofs for immortality, could be seen as no more that reason "running on fumes." In this case, reason has "exceeded its usefulness."

# 8

## Science or Religion?

> *Faith and reason are like two wings on which the human spirit rises to the contemplation of truth; and God has placed in the human heart a desire to know the truth—in a word, to know himself—so that, by knowing and loving God, men and women may also come to the fullness of truth about themselves*
>
> —John Paul II, *Fides Et Ratio*

> *It is impossible to use electric light and the wireless and to avail ourselves of modern medical and surgical discoveries, and at the same time to believe in the New Testament world of spirits and miracles*
>
> —Rudolf Bultmann, *Kerygma and Myth*

THE TWO quotations shown above seem to capture some of the tensions within religious faith today—particularly Christianity. At least within the Catholic tradition, there has been an attempt to show how beliefs that are held by faith do not conflict with beliefs reached through the use of what has become known as "natural reason." The classical position on this was articulated by St. Thomas Aquinas in the thirteenth century.

Aquinas held that some of the deliverances of faith could also be proven by natural reason, while some of them could not. Yet, even in the case of those items which reason could not prove by itself, it could at least be shown that they did not directly contradict other truths well-established by natural reason. More will be said about this position later in the chapter, as well as the meaning of key terms like "natural reason." However, we are faced today with the full-fledged reality of the modern empirical sciences (physics, chemistry, biology, etc.) and with the astounding leaps in technological capability that has accompanied them. In fact, it is not too much to say that we owe a never-before-seen quality of life to these developments in the empirical sciences and in technology. Everything from a plentiful food supply to cutting-edge medical technology. Given these scientifically-enabled revolutions in human experience, it is hardly surprising that many people would assume that every other approach to knowledge and reality preceding what has become known as "the scientific revolution" would pale in comparison. Indeed, some of the early spokesmen for the "new science" sensed that they were standing at the dawn of a new age of progress and knowledge. For example, Francis Bacon, in his *Novum Organum*, writing as an enthusiastic devotee of this new science said, "The sciences we now possess are merely systems for the nice ordering and setting forth of things already invented, not methods of invention or directions for new works." It would be the task of the new empirical sciences to give this new method of invention and progress.

Inevitably, the question arises, what is the connection, if any, between these empirical sciences and the religious world-view, as it has come down to us in Christianity? The world-view of the empirical sciences seems to be quite different from the Christian world-view. How do we account for this? Does one of them have to be "wrong"? Unfortunately, many educated people who have noticed this situation have tended to assume that one of the two must be mistaken. Most often it is science that is taken to be "right" while religion is dismissed as "wrong" and perhaps out of date. But there are a few religious types who would conclude, against popular opinion, that it is the other way around—one thinks, for instance, of the much-publicized "Scopes Trial" where a Christian understanding of the creation-story in Genesis was set up as an alternative to the account given by evolutionary theory. Such attempts to ignore the other viewpoint are unhelpful and tend to leave more questions unanswered than problems solved. It will be argued in this chapter that the traditional balance between faith and reason can be maintained in the more generalized confrontation between science and religion. In the first section I will outline the traditional Catholic position on the relation between faith and reason, as it emerged into full expression in the thirteenth century. In the second section I will ask why it is that science is viewed as irreconcilable with the Christian standpoint (it will come down to: (i) a confusion between methodological and ontological reductionism; and (ii) as a result of the first, a misunderstanding of the nature of reason, and human experience). Finally, in the third section I will make some suggestions as to how Christianity should approach the scientific world/viewpoint. This is an approach which refuses to unduly narrow the scope of human reason and experience, but is nevertheless ready to recognize "the facts" when they are established. As will be seen, not only does theology struggle to articulate some of the basic features of the religious standpoint; scientists also struggle to articulate some of the basic features of how their research connects with reality.

I

A useful point at which to begin a summary of the Catholic position on faith and reason is St. Paul's famous Areopagus speech (in Acts 17). For while it is Paul's explicit intention to bring the message of Christianity to the Athenians, he skillfully makes use of an already-existent shrine dedicated to "an unknown god." Paul simply declares to the Athenians that "what therefore you worship as unknown, this I proclaim to you." Indeed, part of his strategy involves finding common ground between Christianity and the educated Athenians listening to him (we are told that the crowd includes stoics and epicureans), and then claiming that this common ground is better explained and illuminated given the *full* world-picture that the Christian vision can offer. To this end, St. Paul quotes a line from a Greek poet that supposedly would resonate even with Christians: "In him we live and move and have our being."[1] Regardless of how successful this attempt was it was significant because it represented an effort to show that the Christian faith need not be seen as destroying whatever is good in preexisting cultures. Instead it *builds* upon them, completes them. Although some have accused this strategy of "compromising" the Christian message, others have claimed that Paul was "proffering a fundamentally Christian worldview while clothing it in the contemporary idiom."[2] It is this latter interpretation that I feel is correct.

There is another point to make in this regard. It might seem as though the business of finding common ground—even with philosophers—is no more than a useful technique, which may or may not be met with success.[3] However, there is more to it than this. One could make a good case that as Christianity began to come to terms with the *universal* scope of its message, and to break out of the strict observance of all Jewish customs,[4]

---

1. Marilyn McCord Adams points out that this passage from Epimenides the Cretan, was "an attempt to meet philosophers on their own turf." From "Philosophy and the Bible: The Areopagus Speech," *Faith and Philosophy*, vol. 9, no. 2, (April 1992), 135–51; 137.

2. Dustin Salter, "Some Brief Ruminations on Areopagus *(Acts 17)*, http://old.thirdmill.org/paul/areopagus.asp/category/life, 1.

3. We are told in the same passage from *Acts*, that St. Paul did not meet with great success in this particular case.

4. See, for example, the description of "the council of Jerusalem" (*Acts 15*).

there was a need for a "vehicle" of some sort, which would allow people with no inkling of Jewish tradition to see the relevance of Christianity in their lives. In a certain sense, the faculty of "reason" answers this call. Since reason can be seen as the "universal nature" of man, it appears to line up nicely with the "universal message" of Christianity. By somehow connecting the Christian message to a "rational appeal/foundation," people everywhere, in virtue of their native reason, would be able to find a connection with the Christian message. One would only need to show that people everywhere, in virtue of their reason, are looking for truth. Christianity claims to speak to this need, and to fulfill it. At any rate, something along these lines helps to show that there was (and is) more than a passing connection between the emerging Christian faith and the demands of reason (embodied emblematically in "philosophy").[5] It will take centuries before this connection is formally articulated in a coherent fashion.

There is a long passage of time before we reach the thirteenth century when Thomas Aquinas gave what was perhaps the clearest portrayal of the way in which faith and reason relate to each other. Up until this point it could not be claimed that there was a harmonious balance between the two. Instead, it became clear in the ongoing centuries of medieval Christendom, that the more theology attempted to illuminate sacred doctrine, and the more that reason attempted to expand the scope and focus of logic and dialectic, the less clear the relationship between them became. Speaking of how this relationship between faith and reason appeared in the eleventh century, one writer comments that "on each side there

5. In his "Regensburg Address," Joseph Ratzinger dwells on this point at some length, arguing explicitly against a view which would attempt to separate faith from reason. We must, he says, see "the profound harmony between what is Greek in the best sense of the word and the biblical understanding of faith in God . . . resulting in a mutual enrichment . . . decisive for the birth and spread of Christianity." http://www.vatican.va/holy_father/benedict_xvi/speeches/2006/september/documents/hf_ben-xvi_spe_20060912_university-regensburg_en.html Ratzinger traces the influence further back into the Old Testament, for example, in the wisdom literature.

was a pronounced tendency to extremism. The exponents of dialectic showed little or no awareness of reason's limits, in applying it to nearly all the truths of dogma; as a reaction, its opponents virtually denied reason any place in faith at all."[6] This was hardly in line with the original hopes for a meeting of faith and reason that seem to have been present in Paul's mind. Matters were not helped at the beginning of the thirteenth century when the entire corpus of Aristotle's works became available again, along with a number of commentaries written by illustrious Muslim philosophers. The problem was that some of Aristotle's doctrines, as well as the way in which they had been interpreted, seemed to be ill-suited to Christian teaching. To take just one example, Aristotle held that the world was eternal; whereas Christianity taught that it had been created in time by God, i.e., had a beginning. In themselves, these points of disagreement could hardly have challenged Christian faith in any significant way. However, most of the Christian philosophers and theologians who read Aristotle were overwhelmed by the power of his mind, and by the inescapable impression that he could not be wrong. One way of dealing with the difficulties here, inspired by Siger of Brabant, was to advocate a "dual truth theory," whereby "what was true in philosophy might be false in theology."[7] It should be clear that this can be no more than a *modus vivendi*, and an ill-fated one at that. For if both the Word of God/revelation and the world of nature come from the same God, then it would seem to be impossible for either to be ultimately incompatible with the other—otherwise God (Truth) would contradict himself.[8]

6. Gordon Leff, *Medieval Thought. St. Augustine to Ockham* (Harmondsworth, Middlesex: Penguin Books Ltd, 1968), 91.

7. D.J.B. Hawkins, *A Sketch of Mediaeval Philosophy* (New York: Sheed & Ward, 1947), 65.

8. This kind of insight was already a part of the tradition by the thirteenth century and can be traced, for example, to St. Augustine's *De Genesi ad Litteram*. "Beginning with the principle that truth is self-consistent, St. Augustine ruled out a priori any real contradiction between the data of revelation, true by definition in the light of their source, and the equally true data of observation and conclusions of true reasoning." From A.C. Crombie,

## THINKING GOD

So how should apparently-conflicting claims of truth be brought together? How should one attempt to reconcile passages of scripture which seem to contradict what philosophical reason is telling us? To begin with, the term "natural reason" needs to be clarified, as this is the term most often used to convey the efforts of traditional philosophy. It seems to mean something like "unaided by special revelation." That is, what reason would be able to establish without any knowledge of what God had revealed of himself through scripture and religious communities, etc. In attempting to come to terms with these very problems St. Thomas Aquinas says, "Some truths about God exceed all the ability of the human reason. Such is the truth that God is triune. But there are some truths which the natural reason also is able to reach. Such are that God exists, that He is one, and the like."[9] Aquinas goes on to make some qualifications. Even in the cases where natural reason is capable of proving something (e.g., the existence of God), it is still appropriate that such truths should be made known by way of revelation, that is, in scripture. For not everyone is capable of philosophical reasoning, and truths of this importance to human life must be more adequately disseminated. Aquinas also feels that while there are truths of faith which clearly go beyond what natural reason is capable of grasping/proving, it is not irrational or irresponsible to believe in them. In fact, he claims, the whole impetus of natural reason in its inquiries seems to be aiming for something which it is incapable of adequately delivering. Natural reason (along with all other human activities) seems to be geared towards helping human beings reach happiness,[10] but the latter is never fully achieved. On principle, therefore, there cannot be any cogent objection to a truth that claims to exceed human reason (and which makes

---

*Medieval and Early Modern Science,* vol. I, (New York: Anchor Books, 1959), 59.

9. *Summa Contra Gentiles,* Book One, ("On the Truth of the Catholic Faith"), trans. Anton C. Pegis (New York: Image Books, 1955), Ch. 3, 63.

10. For instance, Aristotle, in the *Nicomachean Ethics,* puts intellectual contemplation down as an integral part of the fulfilled life.

claims about how to reach ultimate human happiness).[11] This is not yet to claim that it must be *true*—only that it is not "irrational" to hold to such revealed truths, precisely because they speak to real human needs.

But there remains the original difficulty about truths of natural reason, which appear to undermine or contradict the truths of revelation. At a general level, Aquinas accepts the "one truth" position mentioned above. According to this position, there cannot be any real contradiction in our system of truths, since they all come from the Truth itself, which cannot contradict itself. But how does this work out at a more particular, detailed level? Supposing that we have a deliverance of natural reason claiming to be undeniably true, and yet which directly contradicts revealed teaching? Aquinas clearly sticks to his one truth theory, claiming that "whatever arguments are brought forward against the doctrines of faith are conclusions incorrectly derived from the first and self-evident principles imbedded in nature. Such conclusions do not have the force of demonstration; they are arguments that are either probable or sophistical. And so, there exists the possibility to answer them."[12] Of course, the possibility of "answering" these arguments against the faith does not always amount to a direct proof of the faith. Aquinas repeats that "our intention should not be to convince our adversary by arguments; it should be to answer his arguments against the truth."[13]

Just how adequate is Aquinas' position here? It seems to depend on the scenario that a conclusion of natural reason is itself not properly demonstrated or plausible. But, to push this question to its ultimate level, what if the claims of natural reason, in a given case, *were* demonstrative, or such that to refuse acquiescence would be "heroically irrational"?[14] If a direct conflict with a truth

11. *Summa Contra Gentiles* Book One, Ch. 6, 71–74.
12. Ibid., Ch. 7, 75.
13. Ibid., Ch. 9, 77.
14. There have been figures in the tradition who have taken such a stance,

of faith arose in that case, then what should our response be? I believe that in such a case, Aquinas, representing the classical position on faith and reason, would claim that the "conflict" is illusory. In other words, he would stick by the one truth theory. But instead of arguing that natural reason has erred, he would claim that the truth of faith has been "incorrectly interpreted" by us. Since it is impossible for revealed truth to be false, if there is any reputed conflict between revealed truth and naturally-reasoned truth, it can only mean that we have done a poor job of understanding the meaning of the revealed truth.

An example might make this clearer. As the theory of evolution becomes more and more sophisticated, and more and more evidential support is discovered, it becomes, if not "contradictory," at least irrational to deny its truth. However, for a long time many Christians thought that it could not be correct, since it seemed to contradict the account of creation given in the book of Genesis. The obvious response, along the lines sketched above, would be to say that the conflict was only apparent. Confusion arose because Genesis had been interpreted as something like a "scientific" explanation or an "historical sequence of events." Instead of this interpretation, we should rather see the Genesis story as a metaphorical, pictorial, and even beautiful attempt to say that all things come from God. Some people will feel uncomfortable with this alteration in the meaning of a religious belief—perhaps it will even be viewed as a watering-down of the original understanding. Yet this is precisely an objection that needs to be rejected if we are to gain an adequate understanding of the relationship between faith and reason. For regardless of whether we question the facts that are set up against the faith or refine our interpretation of our faith in light of the undeniable facts; in both cases, the truth of faith behaves as a "horizon" within which facts themselves take on an

---

usually referred to as "fideistic." Tertullian long ago set the tone for this kind of response, with his defiant retort, "Credo quia absurdum est" (I believe *because* it is absurd).

importance and significance for human life. This is obvious in the case where "the facts" are challenged in order to hold onto a particular viewpoint of faith—for this viewpoint and its interpretation is believed important enough to challenge the alleged facts. It is less obvious when the interpretation of faith has to be refined. In the latter case, however, there would still have to be an essential kernel of meaning/significance, which remained in the reinterpretation. Otherwise one could not speak of a "re-interpretation" at all—the meaning of the faith position would simply have been lost.

Be this as it may, a version of this position on the relation between faith and reason has come down to us today, and represents a mainstream account. As can be seen from the evolution example, it is not too difficult to apply it to questions and challenges arising from contemporary science. Science would therefore be classed as a form of "reason." However, this is where we need to tread cautiously. For it is often supposed that the world of contemporary science and its methodology cannot be equated with what was considered "rational procedure" prior to the advent of modern science. In fact, it would be claimed by many that the faith-reason compromise, when seen as a faith-science compromise, has all but evacuated the realm of faith of anything firmly reliable as far as knowledge goes. On this view, faith would, at best, represent a comforting realm of inspired feeling where the individual can take refuge from the harsh facts of reality, paradigmatically revealed by science. So serious is this view that it represents the main force behind the common conception that one must choose between scientific and religious viewpoints about reality. And yet, it is an incorrect view, arising from a misconception of the nature of reason, the nature of reality, and therefore of scientific procedure. In the next section, an effort will be made to explain how this is the case.

## II

(i) *Reason divided*: the first task in understanding the view that science is incompatible with religion is largely historical. As historians of both philosophy and science are constantly pointing out, there were at first no neatly demarcated areas for what we have come to think of today as the separate realms of "science" and "philosophy." "Reason" stood for a unified endeavor, which, while it might have taken different approaches here and there, was ultimately a cohesive and coherent body of truths. Thus, investigations into the structure of the physical world could go hand-in-hand with proofs for the existence of God. All of this changed at the dawn of the scientific revolution, and as one commentator put it, "If we are asked to name the man who did most to start physical science on the triumphant course which lasted for nearly three hundred years, we must answer: Galileo Galilei (1564–1642)."[15] For our purposes, it is not just his indisputable scientific brilliance which is of interest, but rather his central approach to reality and what he viewed as the new—and much superior—*rational* method. At the most general level, there is no immediate concern for the unity of reason (although this would be an additional boon). Instead, "each fact is accepted as it stands with no desire to make it fit into a universal pre-ordained whole."[16] To further round out the rejection of this traditionally unifying conception of reason that had been prevalent up until that point, our commentator says, "Mediaeval Scholasticism was rational, modern science is in essence empirical, accepting brute facts whether they seem reasonable or not."[17]

Yet, one must go further in order to see the radical change in the conception of rational approach that men like Galileo brought about. For it is not just that they had a changed conception of

---

15. William Cecil Dampier, *A Shorter History of Science* (New York: Meridian Books, 1957), 61.
16. Ibid.
17. Ibid.

reason itself. Rather was it the case that their changed conception of reason was a response to a changed conception of what reality was like. Before the scientific revolution, nature had been a grand hierarchical scale of reality[18] within which man found his place, and which practically exuded a divine presence. The new science tended to "reduce" nature to the barest physical attributes (like figure and extension), and to develop a method based on the mathematical description of movement (loco-motion). As one writer puts it, "The main difference between the old and the new philosophy of nature lay not in particular discoveries but in conflicting notions about *demonstration* and *method*."[19] This new approach and new conception of reality "goes hand in hand with a philosophical rejection of the Aristotelian notion of prime matter and a description of bodies exclusively in function of extension and local motion."[20] Looking at these changes, it is still not clear how or why they should have had such an enormous impact on the conception of rational method, and ultimately, on the position of man in reality. In truth, there was no *a priori* reason why they should have proved problematic.[21] To see the far-reaching consequences of Galileo's approach, it is necessary to briefly mention the doctrine of "primary" and "secondary" qualities. In a nutshell, primary qualities would be the ones that Galileo was interested in—they are features such as number, figure, and position. These primary qualities are viewed as inseparable from the objects themselves.

18. The classic treatment of this pervasive worldview, in English, can be found in Arthur Lovejoy, *The Great Chain of Being* (Cambridge, MA: Harvard University Press, 1964).

19. James Collins, *A History of Modern European Philosophy* (Milwaukee: The Bruce Publishing Company, 1954), 76.

20. Ibid.

21. Ernst Cassirer pointed out that Galileo himself seems to have thought there need be no conflict with the traditional religious viewpoint at first, but that he had failed to appreciate the radical alteration in methodology that lay at the heart of the new science. See Cassirer's *The Philosophy of the Enlightenment*, trans. Fritz C.A. Koelln and James P. Pettegrove (Boston: Beacon Press, 1951), 37–49.

Furthermore, they are the kind of qualities directly utilized and described by the new scientific approach. Secondary qualities, on the other hand, are features like taste, smell, touch, etc. They may be distantly caused by the primary qualities, but they have no reality outside of the subject, or human perceiver. At first glance, this appears to be a fairly innocuous standpoint. But the central point for our purposes is that many of the qualities that we take to be most primordial to our experience of reality are rendered literally "secondary," and thus excluded from the foundational picture of reality. As one intellectual historian puts it, "We have the first stage in the reading of man quite out of the real and primary realm."[22] Not only this, but "along with this exultation of the external world as more primary and more real, went an attribution to it of greater dignity and value."[23] It is not very difficult to see how this could ultimately affect our view of the human being. Since our bodies can be viewed as possessing primary qualities, it would seem that only our physical, biological selves, so to speak, could have the scientifically-respectable objective aspect. In other words, most if not all of the attributes which had been religiously significant for humanity—freedom of will, immortal soul, etc.—can no longer be spoken of according to the new paradigm for knowledge (if they can be spoken of at all). Whether or not one has freedom of will, for instance, would have to bow to the new primary level of reality. It would then be parsed out as a series of observations about whether or not one was physically impeded in one's loco-motion.[24] Unsurprisingly, "it was inevitable that in these circumstances man should now appear to be outside of the real world . . . man begins to appear for the first time in the history of thought as an irrelevant

---

22. E.A. Burtt, *The Metaphysical Foundations of Modern Science* (New York: Doubleday Anchor Books, 1954), 89.

23. Ibid., 90.

24. An illustration of such a reinterpretation of freedom can be found in Thomas Hobbes' *Leviathan*.

*Science or Religion?*

spectator and insignificant effect of the great mathematical system which is the substance of reality."[25]

(ii) *Reason re-grounded*: In the above, reference was made primarily to what is known as "classical physics." Anybody with a cursory knowledge of the history of science will be aware that the world of contemporary physics has broken out of this particular paradigm of reason. Furthermore, the scientific view of humanity has posed challenges from the area of biology too, in particular from the perspective of evolution. But in both cases it seems to be true that the "scientific models" are not easily reconciled with the kinds of things that religious people want to say. Whether one is a physicist or a biologist, one will eventually have to ask how one's scientific picture of reality meets up (if it does) with the picture of reality that religious people are offering. The question at this point in the discussion is what are we to do about this confrontation of viewpoints? The traditional Catholic standpoint, as has been observed, is to try to reconcile reason-science with faith. This means that science and its claims can neither be ignored as irrelevant, nor attacked as falsehoods. But does any other way of proceeding remain? What would a contemporary attempt to apply the traditional faith-reason compromise look like?

Returning for a moment to the point made at the outset of this section, scientific practice *did* eventually separate itself off from philosophy, despite their initial inseparability. However, as Peter Dear, a professor of science and technology studies, has shown in a recent book,[26] it is virtually impossible to firmly distinguish the first-hand practice of science from the "natural philosophy" that accompanies it. That is, running parallel with the advances and achievements of science are a number of standard explanations of what reality must be like in order for those achievements to occur. And the interesting point about these natural philosophical

---

25. Ibid.
26. Peter Dear, *The Intelligibility of Nature. How Science Makes Sense of the World* (Chicago: University of Chicago Press, 2006).

explanations is that they are extremely changeable. Dear gives the example of the erstwhile theory of "material ether," which had been popular amongst physicists before the presentation of Einstein's special theory of relativity. It had been thought necessary in order to explain phenomena like light and electromagnetism.[27] We might also take the primary-secondary qualities theory as a further illustration, itself thought necessary to explain the primacy of mathematical reason. Now it is not being said, through these examples, that the natural philosophy component of scientific practice is useless. Rather, that "the practical efficacy of scientific theories, what can be called their 'instrumentality,' is a component of science distinguishable from its natural philosophy."[28] Well, it might be asked, where does this land us? Are we to discard any attempt on the part of scientists at natural philosophy? That would be extreme indeed. Perhaps a safer lesson to be learnt is that we must accept that the "context of discovery" and the "context of justification" are much closer than was at first suspected. That is, the historical circumstances, as well as prejudicial beliefs of a given period in history, which were in place at the time of any significant scientific discovery/advance, form an ineradicable part of how those discoveries are explained and justified. Thus, as scientific practice is inseparable from historical development, one can never seem to say with any degree of finality what a given advance/discovery actually *means*, *vis-à-vis* the larger questions about our reality. Pragmatically speaking, this need pose no threat to scientific practice, as the effectiveness in coping with reality, making accurate predictions, and so on, remains unaffected.[29] Scientists,

27. Ibid., 4.
28. Ibid., 5.
29. Nevertheless, this kind of view *was* seen as a threat to the rationality of scientific procedure by many theorists, who worried about a descent into relativism. For a short discussion of these issues, and how they affect contemporary philosophy of science, see Alexander Bird, "The Historical Turn in the Philosophy of Science," in Psillos Stathis & Curd Martin, Eds., *The Routledge Companion to Philosophy of Science* (New York: Routledge, 2008).

even granted the seemingly built-in historicity of their self-understanding, can perfectly well get on with their work—perhaps also offering their best attempt at a reflective interpretation of that work, but not worrying too much if it should be found to be incomplete/unfinalized in some respect.[30]

The point of the preceding paragraph was to draw attention to a potential complacency in how the achievements of science are sometimes viewed. It is *not* obvious how the stupendous results of scientific discovery and understanding affect our picture of reality. So, perhaps the first conclusion we can reach about the contemporary science-faith problem, is that if religion is sometimes unclear on its connection with reality, so too is science. Yet, this conclusion, true as it is, does not take us much further with our original question. If so much of human experience that was traditionally associated with religious faith has been read out of the scientific picture of reality, then what is to be said about this? Part of the answer is forthcoming from what has already been said. For it seems undeniable that, for example, the distinction between primary and secondary qualities that launched the self-interpretation of scientific practice at the dawn of the scientific revolution, is a highly questionable one. There seems to be no reason why the culmination of the early-modern period in the history of science, in the Newtonian system, needs to have been saddled with such a distinction at all. The fact that it *was*, simply confirms the close alliance between the contexts of discovery and justification. But the recognition that this primary-secondary distinction is somewhat superfluous, does more than this. For if, as has been claimed, it was

---

30. This insight into the operations of science seems to lie behind part of the pragmatist movement in philosophy, and its attempt to reconceptualize the actual procedures of scientific practice, as opposed to the actual self-understanding often offered by scientists of those procedures. As John Dewey said, "From the standpoint of scientific inquiry nothing is more fatal to its right to obtain acceptance than a claim that its conclusions are final and hence incapable of a development that is other than mere quantitative extension." From *Reconstruction in Philosophy* (Boston: Beacon Press, 1948), xvi.

responsible for the original view of large portions of human experience being read out of significant scientific explanation; then it behooves us to reconsider the connection between our human experience of reality, and what is going on in scientific investigation.

As a matter of fact, such a reconsideration has been a part of the philosophical landscape for some time, over and above the efforts of the afore-mentioned pragmatist school. But before we look more closely at these efforts, I would like to begin with a similar line of thought from a well-known scientist, lest it be thought that only philosophers are speaking of this need to recontextualize. The physicist Werner Heisenberg, writing of the connection between modern/contemporary notions of physics and how they have changed from the classical Newtonian model, admits that the latter was "so narrow and rigid that it was difficult to find a place in it for many concepts of our language that had always belonged to its very substance, for instance, the concepts of mind, of the human soul or of life."[31] This much can be gathered from our discussion so far. But Heisenberg wants to know about the connection between the concepts and human experience which are our natural heritage, and the precise language of science/physics. He says that "one of the most important features of the development and analysis of modern physics is the experience that the concepts of natural language, vaguely defined as they are, seem to be more stable in the expansion of knowledge than the precise terms of scientific language, derived as an idealization from only limited groups of phenomena. This is in fact not surprising since the concepts of natural language are formed by the immediate connection with reality; they represent reality."[32] In claiming that "natural language" touches reality, Heisenberg is clearly distancing himself from the view that so much of human experience is *secondary*, and cut off

---

31. Werner Heisenberg, "Science and Culture," in *Science, Faith and Man. European Thought Since 1914*, ed. Wagar, W. Warren (New York: Harper & Row, 1968), 24–25.

32. Ibid., 26.

from the so-called *primary* aspects of reality. This is not to deny the importance or insight of scientific practice. On the contrary, he says only that "any understanding must be based finally upon the natural language because it is only there that we can be certain to touch reality . . . in this way modern physics has perhaps opened the door to a wider outlook on the relation between the human mind and reality."[33] Indeed, he says that "our attitude toward concepts like mind or the human soul or life or God will be different from that of the nineteenth century because these concepts belong to the natural language and have therefore immediate connection with reality."[34]

The central point to keep in mind here, is that the original rupture in the meaning of "reason" at the dawn of the scientific revolution was a little too hasty in its systematic marginalization of large areas of human experience, previously thought to fall within the ambit of "reason." By appealing to a base-line level of natural human experience, Heisenberg is in a sense both reintegrating the full meaning of human experience, as well as re-grounding scientific practice as a specific "growth"/development taken from this original experience. And yet what he describes as a more adequate approach to science, based on the entire extent of human experience, has been some time in the making already. For instance, in the systems of the great German Idealists (especially Hegel); in the advent of a neo-scholastic philosophy, which explicitly addresses itself to modern science and it presuppositions;[35] and in the modern phenomenological movement pioneered by Edmund Husserl. In fact, it is the latter school of phenomenology that has survived to the present day, and whose many and varied disciples have investigated everything from the nature of physical perception to

---

33. Ibid., 28.
34. Ibid., 27.
35. This movement was spearheaded by Cardinal Mercier, at the Institute of Philosophy, in the Catholic University of Louvain, around the beginning of the twentieth century.

the nature of human relationships, sharing nothing more than a firm methodological conviction that "experience" is far more open than the natural sciences traditionally assumed. Edmund Husserl himself claimed that "all natural science is naïve in regard to its point of departure. The nature that it will investigate is for it simply there."[36] Husserl does not deny that the empirical sciences do manage to articulate a form of their own critique and analysis of experience, but he insists that it is based on a more primordial experience, requiring its own method of investigation. As he puts it, "As long as we remain within natural science and think according to its point of view, a completely different critique of experience is still possible and indispensable, a critique that places in question all experience as such and the sort of thinking proper to empirical science."[37] Especially at the end of this quotation we see that Husserl is more intent on properly "grounding" the empirical sciences than on attacking their achievements *per se*.

Whether or not one agrees with Heisenberg or with the phenomenological approach, it is arguable that one of the most promising ways forward, in regard to the science-religion debate, is *via* a reappraisal of the meaning of human experience. For it is experience in one form or another, that both science and religion claim to make their starting-point. To this degree, it is unlikely that either side could be completely wrong. After all if people claim to have *experienced* the reality of something, then it is highly unlikely that it can be dismissed out of hand—least of all by an approach which deliberately filters out aspects of experience which it deems inconvenient/irrelevant to its approach.

---

36. Edmund Husserl, "Philosophy as Rigorous Science," in *Husserl. Shorter Works*, trans. Quentin Lauer, ed. McCormick Peter and Elliston Frederick (Notre Dame: University of Notre Dame Press, 1981), 171.

37. Ibid., 172.

## III

At this point it is useful to raise again the problem that guided the writing of this chapter. Have we in any way come closer to resolving the problem of a potential antagonism between scientific reason and religious faith? Can the traditional Catholic solution to the problem of faith and reason still hold good? Beginning with the second of these questions, I believe that the traditional position on faith and reason *does* hold good, although it may be more difficult to see how. One way of looking at it is that instead of figuring out the relationship only in terms of "propositional content" (e.g., doctrinal definitions vs. scientific observation statements), one can configure the relationship in terms of how both approaches express aspects of human experience. Thus, if we are to proceed along the lines suggested above, should a scientific statement about how to understand experience openly seem to negate an aspect of experience as interpreted by religion; then that would be grounds to suspect the full accuracy of the scientific statement. For example, if the experience of love seems to carry more than can be unpacked by a statement about how brains and nervous systems work; it is just as legitimate to claim that the explanation is at fault, as it is to deny any further meaning to love experiences. After all, both claims attempt to base themselves on experience, which is prior to reflection.

Obviously, this is not a ready-made guide for how to reach informed reflective decisions. But it does open up the possibility for a fruitful dialogue that could take us further than the current "standoff" seems to allow. For the real fear of religious people in this regard seems to be that science will come up with a systematic set of statements that will somehow negate/disprove all of the most deeply cherished beliefs that religious people hold about human experience. Our human values, as expressed in religious faith, would turn out to be completely ungrounded and illusory. Perhaps it is time to shed this fear. Any talk about what has been proved/

unproved must ultimately be referred back to human experience. And at that level, either you experience something or you do not. Religious attestations seem to point towards the former possibility.

www.ingramcontent.com/pod-product-compliance
Lightning Source LLC
Chambersburg PA
CBHW050834160426
43192CB00010B/2024